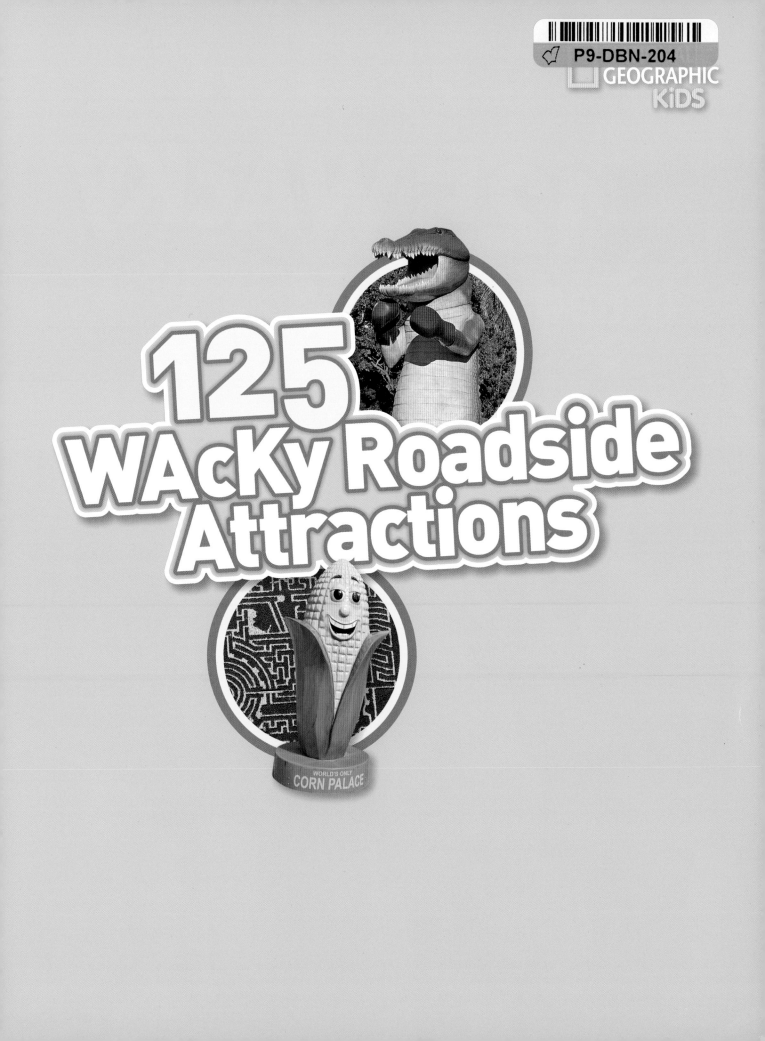

NATIONAL GEOGRAPHIC KiDS

125
WAcKy Roadside
Attractions

WORLD'S ONLY
CORN PALACE

125 WACKy
Roadside Attractions

Contents

Introduction

HAVE YOU EVER
spent the night in an elephant or driven through a huge tree? Welcome to the road-onkulous, hilarious, and sometimes spooky world of wacky roadside attractions! Ever since the car was invented in the late 1800s, roadside businesses have been trying to catch the eye of behind-the-wheel consumers as they zoom past. Cruise through these pages and find 125 of National Geographic Kids' favorite places to stop when you're out on the road, traveling the world.

Drop in at a hair museum and slow down while you drive past a wall of chewing gum. Check out a haunted castle or pull over at a farm where you can zip line over alligators. These weird-but-true places are not only fun to read about, but they may also make you laugh or teach you something about history. So prepare to be amazed by these rib-tickling, wonderful, and sometimes creepy stops that are off the beaten path in more ways than one!

page 31

page 66

page 107

page 29

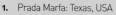

Road Map

1. Prada Marfa: Texas, USA
2. Coral Castle Museum: Florida, USA
3. Happy Rizzi House: Germany
4. Vent Haven Museum: Kentucky, USA
5. Stuart Landsborough's Puzzling World: New Zealand
6. Tunnel of Love: Ukraine
7. Upside-Down House: Poland
8. Green Magic Nature Resort: India
9. Kakslauttanen Arctic Resort: Finland
10. Dog Bark Park Inn B&B: Idaho, USA
11. Gamirasu Cave Hotel: Turkey
12. V8 Hotel: Germany
13. Giraffe Manor: Kenya
14. Tayka Hotel de Sal: Bolivia
15. Magic Mountain Lodge: Chile
16. Burj Al Arab: United Arab Emirates
17. Painted Moose: Canada
18. Bigfoot Statue and Buried A-Frame House: Washington, USA
19. Ruggles Mine: New Hampshire, USA
20. Abita Mystery House: Louisiana, USA
21. Vulcan Tourism and Trek Station: Canada
22. Gnome Reserve and Wild Flower Garden: England, UK
23. Waterwalkerz Ball: Russia
24. Larry the Lobster: Australia
25. Weeki Wachee Springs Mermaid Show: Florida, USA
26. Pig Beach: Bahamas, Atlantic Ocean
27. Lucy the Elephant: New Jersey, USA
28. The Blue Whale: Oklahoma, USA
29. St. Augustine Alligator Farm Zoological Park: Florida, USA
30. Queen Connie: Vermont, USA
31. Purple Martin Capital of the US: Illinois, USA
32. Wee'l Turtle: North Dakota, USA
33. Birdhouse Paradise: Indiana, USA
34. Town Built Into Rock: Spain
35. Creepy Gollum: New Zealand
36. Fresh Water Fishing Hall of Fame and Museum: Wisconsin, USA
37. Sam Hill's Stonehenge: Washington, USA
38. Carhenge: Nebraska, USA
39. Dragon Hedge: England, UK
40. Lawn on Roof: Faroe Islands
41. Ben & Jerry's Flavor Graveyard: Vermont, USA
42. European Beard Championships: Austria
43. Guanajuato International Air Balloon Festival: Mexico
44. Mexico City's Summer Celebration: Mexico
45. Outhouse Race: Alaska
46. International Pillow Fight Day: Hungary
47. Flower Parade: Netherlands
48. Flower Festival and Car Parade: Colombia
49. Royal Ascot: England, UK
50. Tiger and Turtle–Magic Mountain: Germany
51. Dinosaur Tracks: Arizona, USA

52. Cabazon Dinosaurs: California, USA
53. Galleries of Paleontology and Comparative Anatomy: France
54. Paris Sewer Museum: France
55. Dennis Severs' House: England, UK
56. Giant Paul Bunyan and Babe the Blue Ox: Minnesota, USA
57. Salt and Pepper Shaker Museum: Tennessee, USA
58. Burlingame Museum of Pez Memorabilia: California, USA
59. Dog Collar Museum: England, UK
60. Shin-Yokohama Ramen Museum: Japan
61. Unclaimed Baggage Center: Alabama, USA
62. International Cryptozoology Museum: Maine, USA
63. The National Mustard Museum: Wisconsin, USA
64. South of the Border: South Carolina, USA
65. Ketchup Bottle Water Tower: Illinois, USA
66. Official Hometown of Superman: Illinois, USA
67. Insectropolis: New Jersey, USA
68. Piano and Violin House: China
69. Old Car City: Georgia, USA
70. Corn Maze: New Jersey, USA
71. Corn Palace: South Dakota, USA
72. Mystery Spot: California, USA
73. Goats on the Roof: Georgia, USA
74. Pike Place Market Gum Wall: Washington, USA

75. Fremont Troll: Washington, USA
76. Two-Story Outhouse: Illinois, USA
77. Duravit Design Center's Extra Large Loo: Germany
78. Leila's Hair Museum: Missouri, USA
79. Keret House: Poland
80. Museum of Bad Art: Massachusetts, USA
81. Santa Claus House: Alaska, USA
82. London Bridge in AZ: Arizona, USA
83. Dinner in the Sky: Belgium
84. Ice-Covered Lighthouse: Michigan, USA
85. Underwater Mailbox: Japan
86. Electric Ladyland: Netherlands
87. Fred Smith's Wisconsin Concrete Park: Wisconsin, USA
88. Catacombs of Paris: France
89. National Museum of Funeral History: Texas, USA
90. Bran Castle: Romania
91. Medieval Crime Museum: Germany
92. Kunstkamera: Russia
93. Old Operating Theatre Museum: England, UK
94. Edinburgh Vaults: Scotland, UK

95. International UFO Museum and Research Center: New Mexico, USA
96. Pops: Oklahoma, USA
97. Brain-Shaped Phone Booth: Brazil
98. Suspended Water Tap: Belgium
99. Enchanted Highway: North Dakota, USA
100. Shobak Castle Tunnels: Jordan
101. Boxing Crocodile: Australia

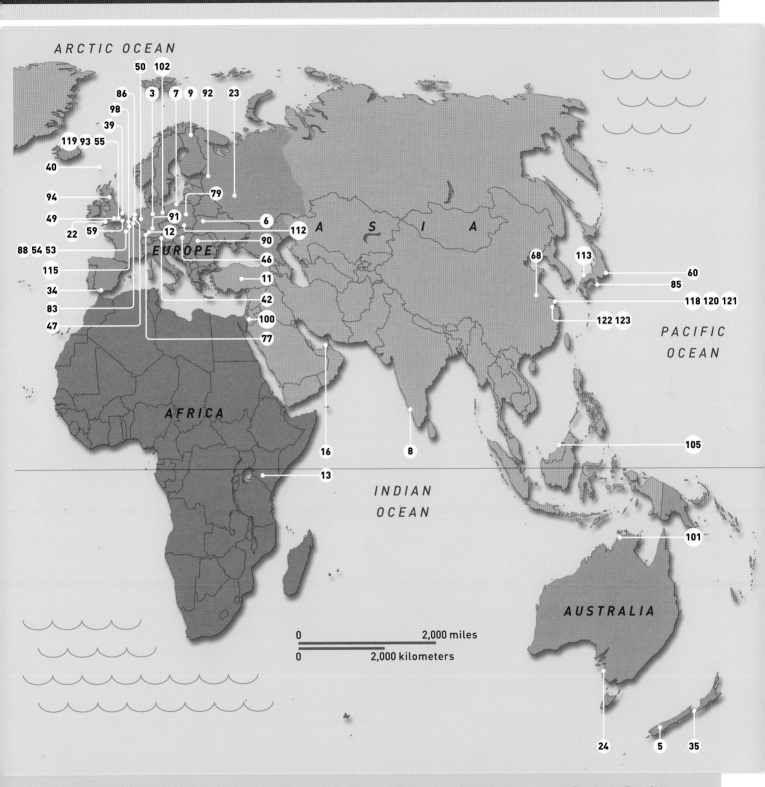

ARCTIC OCEAN

ASIA

EUROPE

AFRICA

PACIFIC OCEAN

INDIAN OCEAN

AUSTRALIA

| 0 | 2,000 miles |
| 0 | 2,000 kilometers |

102. Shop Covered in Bicycles: Germany
103. Polar Bear Swim: Canada
104. Hand of the Desert: Chile
105. Deer Cave: Malaysian Borneo
106. Meteor Crater Visitor Center: Arizona, USA
107. Chandelier Tree: California, USA
108. Masaya Volcano National Park: Nicaragua

109. Kasha-Katuwe, Tent Rocks National Monument: New Mexico, USA
110. Petrified Forest National Park: Arizona, USA
111. Billy Tripp's Mindfield: Tennessee, USA
112. Wieliczka Salt Mine: Poland
113. Eshima Ohashi Bridge: Japan

114. House on the Rock: Wisconsin, USA
115. Braderie de Lille: France
116. Giant Eyeball Sculpture: Texas, USA
117. Roadside America Miniature Villages: Pennsylvania, USA
118. Bund Sightseeing Tunnel: China
119. Traffic Light Tree: England, UK
120. Thames Town: China

121. Scandinavian Town: China
122. Sky City: China
123. Venice Water Town: China
124. San Francisco's Chinatown: California, USA
125. Art Car Museum: Texas, USA

PRADA MARFA

WHAT: DESERT SHOE STORE
WHERE: HIGHWAY 90, WEST TEXAS, U.S.A.

That's no mirage: There really is a luxury shoe and purse store in the middle of nowhere in the Texas desert. Some 30 miles (48 km) outside the tiny town of Marfa stands a sculpture made to resemble one of the fancy Prada shops typically found in big cities like New York City and Tokyo. It's stocked with the Italian designer's shoes and purses, but visitors can only window-shop: There is no working door.

Unveiled in 2005, the sculpture is made from materials that will degrade over time, so the shop will "melt" away.

CORAL CASTLE MUSEUM

The Coral Castle is said to have been sculpted entirely with small hand tools—no heavy machinery allowed!

WHAT: HARD-ROCK STOP
WHERE: HOMESTEAD, FLORIDA, U.S.A.

Come see the incredible castle carved from fossilized remains of teeny-tiny sea creatures! Legend has it that a heartbroken man constructed this fortress and sculpture garden after his fiancée left him at the altar. How exactly he did it is a mystery: He worked under the cover of night and in secret—for 28 years! While walking the grounds, you'll marvel at the massive amount of rock manipulated into features like a rocking chair and a nine-ton (8 t) gate.

HAPPY RIZZI HOUSE

WHAT: HAPPIEST HOUSE EVER
WHERE: BRUNSWICK, GERMANY

Move over, Disney World! This crazy-colorful, cartoon-clad cluster of buildings in Germany claims to be one of the happiest places on Earth. Named for James Rizzi, the American artist who decorated its façade, the house stands out among the traditional surrounding buildings. Though it wasn't a hit with locals at first, people from all over now come to see the silly house that puts a smile on your face.

The eyes of some of the cartoon characters painted on the buildings double as windows.

VENT HAVEN MUSEUM

WHAT: HOUSE FULL OF DUMMIES
WHERE: FORT MITCHELL, KENTUCKY, U.S.A.

You might feel like someone's watching you at this offbeat stop. More than 800 pairs of eyes await you at the world's only museum about the art of ventriloquism. In this type of puppetry, a person "throws" their voice so that it seems to come from a wooden dummy whose mouth they're moving. Tours of the home are offered by appointment May through September. Wonder what the dummies do the rest of the year?

A ventriloquist won the second season of the TV show *America's Got Talent.*

STUART LANDSBOROUGH'S PUZZLING WORLD

WHAT: BRAIN GAMES GALORE
WHERE: WANAKA, NEW ZEALAND

This mind-bending attraction is dedicated to all types of brainteasers. Before tackling its famous "3-D Super Maze," warm up your problem-solving skills with a visit to the tilted towers and rooms filled with optical illusions. Or piece together one of dozens of puzzles atop tables in the café. Before you leave, be sure to take a look—or two—inside the Roman Toilets public restroom to view an epic illusion. And visit the gift shop for all sorts of games to keep you busy for the rest of your road trip.

There are 25 other "Super Mazes" designed by Stuart Landsborough around the world.

TUNNEL OF LOVE

WHAT: SWEET STROLL
WHERE: KLEVAN, UKRAINE
This section of railroad outside the small community of Klevan doubles as a popular place for a romantic stroll. Couples have to be careful to avoid the train that rolls through three times a day, but the walk is said to be worth it. It's rumored that wishes made in the tunnel will later come true. The tunnel's shape isn't maintained by hand. Instead, the train keeps the trees from growing onto the tracks simply by rolling through and clearing its path.

The train that rolls through the tunnel delivers wood to a nearby factory.

UPSIDE-DOWN HOUSE

There are also upside-down houses in China, Germany, Russia, and Austria.

WHAT: TOPSY-TURVY DWELLING
WHERE: SZYMBARK, POLAND

You'll have to stand on your head to get this house to appear right side up! This two-story structure was actually built upside down, and it welcomes visitors via a window near the roof. As you walk around the home, you're actually strolling across ceilings instead of floors. What a trip! After your tour, stop in the nearby hotel to see the world's longest wooden plank, which stretches more than 118 feet (36 m) and was carved from a Douglas fir.

LOONY LODGING

Check into these weird and wonderful hotels that offer guests anything-but-average accommodations!

GREEN MAGIC NATURE RESORT

WHAT: SLEEP IN THE TREES
WHERE: VYTHIRI, INDIA

Riding a pulley-operated lift 86 feet (26 m) to your treetop room is just the start of your adventure. As you look out your open window—there's no glass!—you spy monkeys and birds in the rain forest canopy. Later, you might test your fear of heights by crossing the handmade rope bridge to the main part of the hotel, or just sit on your bamboo bed and read. You don't even have to come down for breakfast—the hotel will send it up on the pulley-drawn "elevator."

KAKSLAUTTANEN

WHAT: ARCTIC RESORT
WHERE: SAARISELKÄ, FINLAND

If you like snow, then this is the place for you! Being able to make it through the night at this chilly igloo hotel definitely ups your personal cool factor (in more ways than one). But even the most adventurous travelers will be glad the hotel provides cold-weather sleeping bags and wool socks: The inside temperature hovers around 25°F (-3.9°C). Just hope that you don't need the bathroom—it's outside. The igloos are open only from December until the end of April. After that, they melt.

DOG BARK PARK INN B&B

WHAT: WORLD'S BIGGEST BEAGLE
WHERE: COTTONWOOD, IDAHO, U.S.A.

This doghouse isn't just for the family pet. Sweet Willy is a 30-foot (9-m)-tall beagle with guest rooms in his belly. Climb the wooden stairs beside his hind leg to enter the door in his side. You can relax in the main bedroom, go up a few steps to the loft in Willy's head, or hang out inside his nose. Gotta "go"? Although you have a full private bathroom in your quarters, there's also a toilet in the 12-foot (3.7-m)-tall fire hydrant outside.

GAMIRASU CAVE HOTEL

WHAT: UNDERGROUND ACCOMMODATIONS
WHERE: AYVALI, TURKEY

This is caveman cool! Experience what it was like 5,000 years ago, when people lived in these mountain caves formed by volcanic ash. But your stay will be much more modern. Bathrooms and electricity provide what you expect from a chic hotel, and the white volcanic ash, called *tufa*, keeps the rooms cool, about 65°F (18.3°C) in summer. (Don't worry—there's heat in winter.)

V8 HOTEL

WHAT: CAR LOVER'S LODGE
WHERE: BÖBLINGEN, GERMANY
Have you ever woken up in a Volkswagen Beetle or in the middle of a sunny race track? Road trip through Germany, and you'll have to park overnight at this automotive fantasyland. Catch a few z's before you hit Germany's famously fast Autobahn in the morning.

The V8 Hotel's drive-thru cinema-themed room comes complete with a night sky, classic movies, and a bed made out of a converted Cadillac Coupe de Ville.

GIRAFFE MANOR

WHAT: A REALLY *WILD* HOTEL
WHERE: NAIROBI, KENYA
Picture this: You're sitting down for breakfast at the Giraffe Manor hotel when you spot the long neck of a giraffe poking through the window next to you. That's no, uh, stretch of your imagination: Dining with the friendly animals is all part of the experience at this stately resort located on the outskirts of Kenya's capital. A herd of endangered Rothschild giraffes roams the hotel grounds, usually visiting the sunroom every morning and evening in the hopes of snagging a tasty treat from guests. Their favorite eats? Special pellets made from dried grass, corn, and molasses.

A family of warthogs and more than 100 species of birds also call the 12-acre (5-ha) resort home.

TAYKA HOTEL DE SAL

WHAT: A SALTY STAY
WHERE: TAHUA, BOLIVIA

You've stayed at hotels made of brick or wood, but salt? That's something few can claim. Tayka Hotel de Sal is made totally of salt—including the beds (though you'll sleep on regular mattresses and blankets). The hotel sits on the Salar de Uyuni, a prehistoric dried-up lake that's the world's biggest salt flat. Builders use the salt from the 4,633-square-mile (12,000-sq-km) flat to make the bricks, and they glue them together with a paste of wet salt that hardens when it dries. When rain starts to dissolve the hotel, the owners just mix up more salt paste to strengthen the bricks.

MAGIC MOUNTAIN LODGE

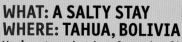

WHAT: VOLCANO-INSPIRED INN
WHERE: PUERTO FUY, CHILE

This 66-foot-tall (20 m) hotel looks like a volcano. But instead of lava, a waterfall erupts out of the top and continuously cascades down the sides. Inspired by nearby Mocho Choshuenco volcano and Huilo-Huilo Falls, the lodge draws its waterfall from a local river. (The water returns to the river through a canal.) Want more excitement? The lodge lies in the protected Huilo-Huilo Biological Reserve, a 386-square-mile (1,000-sq-km) rain forest. You can mountain bike or kayak, zoom along the longest zip-line course in South America, or ski year-round on the glacier-covered volcano.

Outside the hotel, guests can soak in hot tubs made from hollow tree stumps.

ACCESO SÓLO HUESPEDES

BURJ AL ARAB

WHAT: LUXURY BY THE SEA
WHERE: DUBAI, UNITED ARAB EMIRATES

No beach? No problem! The builders behind the Burj Al Arab made their own island so that this sail-shaped hotel appears to be cruising 918 feet (280 m) into the Arabian Gulf. This offshore marvel shimmers inside with enough gold leaf to cover more than two professional baseball diamonds. A simulated submarine ride takes you to a seafood restaurant with a giant aquarium. Nearby is the Wild Wadi water park (free for guests).

Some hotel guests get personalized butler service and are chauffeured around in a white Rolls Royce.

PAINTED MOOSE

WHAT: MOOSE GET TATTOOS
WHERE: ONTARIO, CANADA

The moose are loose! Well, kind of. Visitors to Ontario's forests might encounter some fiberglass moose sculptures among the trees. The life-size works of art are just a few of the 326 pieces that once lined the streets of Toronto. Today, the animals are scattered all over the world—some are as far away as Shanghai, China. That's a long trot.

MOOSE CROSSING

BIGFOOT STATUE AND BURIED A-FRAME HOUSE

The 1980 eruption wiped out all signs of life for nearly six square miles (16 sq km).

WHAT: SEE BEASTS AND VOLCANO BLAST DESTRUCTION
WHERE: KID VALLEY, WASHINGTON, U.S.A.

When Mount St. Helens erupted in 1980, it forever changed forests, rivers, and homes near and far. But did the blast bury the region's legendary and little-seen inhabitant, Bigfoot? A 28-foot (8.5-m)-tall statue of the creature stands next to a house half-buried by the massive mudslide triggered by the blast, some 30 miles (48 km) away. On your way to see the still-steaming volcano, pull over and have your picture taken—it may be your only Bigfoot sighting.

Sam Ruggles first mined the mineral mica from this site in 1803. By the 1930s, an estimated $12 million worth of the mineral had been unearthed.

RUGGLES MINE

WHAT: MINE FOR MINERALS
WHERE: GRAFTON, NEW HAMPSHIRE, U.S.A.

You can really dig into this stop! This 200-year-old mine at the top of a mountain is mostly an open pit, but there are also tunnels and cavernous rooms to explore. Rent a hammer or bring your own small tools to chip away at the rock in search of more than 150 types of minerals, including amethyst and garnet. If you come up empty-handed, head to the gift shop to buy minerals mined onsite and other cool items such as crack-your-own geodes. (Open weekends mid-May through mid-June, then daily through mid-October.)

ABITA MYSTERY HOUSE

WHAT: SOUTHERN ODDITIES GALORE
WHERE: ABITA SPRINGS, LOUISIANA, U.S.A.

On your way down to New Orleans, make sure to stop by the Abita Mystery House for some old-fashioned Louisiana charm. Inside the renovated gas station turned museum, you'll find swamp creatures like Buford the Bassigator, a shrine dedicated to Elvis Presley, a UFO crash landing site, and a 30-foot (9-meter)-long animated diorama showcasing fantastical stops along a southern state highway. The museum also boasts large collections of paint-by-number artwork, hot sauces, and pinball machines. Before you hit the road again, press the button on the marble machine to watch marbles roll through a contraption made of Popsicle sticks, hot glue sticks, pinball machine parts, and plumbing supplies.

VULCAN TOURISM AND TREK STATION

WHAT: STAR TREK CAPITAL OF CANADA
WHERE: VULCAN, ALBERTA, CANADA

This tiny prairie town was named for the Roman god of fire, not the *Star Trek* character Spock (who was half-Vulcan, a fictional alien race). However, to attract visitors, the town opened a spaceship-shaped tourist center that also serves as a stop for all things *Star Trek*. Here you can explore more than 800 pieces of memorabilia from the long-running TV show and pick up something far-out for yourself at the Galaxy gift shop. Be sure to don a costume for a photo in front of the green screen that makes you look as though you're actually aboard a spaceship!

A 31-foot (9.5-m)-long spaceship inspired by the *Star Trek* starship U.S.S. *Enterprise* overlooks the highway in town.

GNOME RESERVE AND WILD FLOWER GARDEN

WHAT: PINT-SIZE PEOPLE AND PLANTS
WHERE: NEAR WEST PUTFORD, ENGLAND, U.K.

Step into this rural English reserve and you'll think fairy tales have come true! More than 2,000 gnome and pixie figurines—the world's largest collection—are scattered amid four acres (1.6 hectare) of countryside bursting with flowers, ferns, and other flora. Visitors are encouraged to wear pointy hats (provided at the park's entrance) while they wander the woodland, so they don't scare the gnomes. If after all that walking you work up an appetite, tea, sandwiches, and dessert can be purchased in the kitchen and taken outside to eat at tiny tables. (Open late March through October.)

The world's largest garden gnome, found in Canada, is about half as tall as a gray whale is long!

WATERWALKERZ BALL

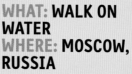

WHAT: WALK ON WATER
WHERE: MOSCOW, RUSSIA
No need for superpowers to walk, spin, or flip on water. At places such as Ostanskinsky Pond (left), you can rent a Waterwalkerz Ball, a gigantic plastic globe that floats on the water's surface. While you're inside, you can romp around—no swimsuit required.

LARRY THE LOBSTER

WHAT: BIG LOBSTER
WHERE: KINGSTON SE, SOUTH AUSTRALIA
Visitors to the Big Lobster restaurant don't need to read a sign to know what kind of food they'll be eating. After all, a 56-foot (17-m)-tall spiny lobster towers over the building. Larry is one of Australia's "Big Things"—a series of giant tourist attractions along the country's roads. With all the attention, Larry and his pals have really come out of their shells.

WEEKI WACHEE SPRINGS

WHAT: LIVE MERMAID SHOW
WHERE: WEEKI WACHEE, FLORIDA, U.S.A.

Sit in a submerged theater and watch as "mermaids" swim before your eyes! The mythical creatures have put on performances in the park's famous springs since 1947. You can explore the crystal clear waters by tour boat, kayak, canoe, and even scuba diving and snorkeling. Or simply go for a swim off the spring's soft, sandy white beaches. Be sure to keep your eyes peeled for manatees—the mammals are said to have inspired mermaid sightings by seafarers for centuries.

Weeki Wachee, known as the "world's only city of live mermaids," has a population of 12.

BRAKE FOR ANIMALS

When you need a break from a long day on the road, we're not *lion*—if you love animals, these destinations are the cat's meow. Stop in and you'll be happier than a pig in mud.

PIG BEACH

WHAT: SWIM WITH THE PIGS

WHERE: EXUMA ISLANDS, THE BAHAMAS, ATLANTIC OCEAN

As if being in paradise wasn't enough, at this beach you can also swim with pigs! A welcome party of swine often swims out to greet visitors approaching by tour boat. The animals have learned that people bring snacks, so they're usually eager to splash in the sea with the guests. After everyone leaves, the pigs seek shade back on the beach. On this uninhabited island, pigs rule!

Other islands around the world have been taken over by animals, including Japan's feline-friendly Cat Island and Assateague Island in Virginia, U.S.A., which is home to wild ponies.

LUCY THE ELEPHANT

Over the years, Lucy has withstood fires, hurricanes, and raging parties in her belly.

WHAT: ELEPHANT-SHAPED BUILDING
WHERE: MARGATE CITY, NEW JERSEY, U.S.A.

No, you're not seeing things. That is a giant elephant on the horizon at the Jersey Shore. Her name is Lucy, and she's not your average pachyderm. All elephants are huge, but Lucy, made of wood and tin, stands 65 feet (19.8 m) high—taller than a six-story building. Built in 1881, Lucy has served as a jumbo-size billboard, a beach house, and a tavern. How do visitors get in? Her 22-foot (6.70-m)-tall legs hide spiral staircases that lead the way.

THE BLUE WHALE

WHAT: CEMENT MARINE MAMMAL
WHERE: CATOOSA, OKLAHOMA, U.S.A.

What a fluke! This cement whale on the side of the road along historic Route 66 was built on a pond by a retired zoologist in 1972. And the 80-foot (24.4-m)-long whale has been a mecca of summer fun ever since. Whether you jump off the giant tail for a swim or picnic in the shade of its big mouth, you're definitely in for a whale of a good time.

Blue whales in the wild can grow longer than a school bus.

ST. AUGUSTINE ALLIGATOR FARM ZOOLOGICAL PARK

WHAT: GET UP CLOSE WITH GATORS
WHERE: ST. AUGUSTINE, FLORIDA, U.S.A.

See Florida's famous alligators from all angles at this fun and freaky farm. At feedings, watch a crowd of hungry gators lunge for lunch dished out by a zookeeper. Hands-on wildlife shows let you hold other animals, like frogs and snakes. And for the truly adventurous, there are two aerial obstacle courses with zip lines that crisscross over the zoo. Cruise above crocodiles and gators and get eye-level with lemurs!

The St. Augustine Alligator Farm is home to other scary animals, including pythons, Komodo dragons, and even a 1,250-pound (567-kg) croc named Maximo!

QUEEN CONNIE OF CONCRETE

WHAT: GIANT PRIMATE
WHERE: BRANDON, VERMONT, U.S.A.

Pull over—it's selfie time! Tourists flock to this toothy royal who reigns over a car dealership. Born and bred in Vermont, the gorilla known as Queen Connie was built from the ground up with more than 20 tons (18 t) of concrete to help sell cars. This pretty primate's scientific name? *Gorilla reinforcei concretei.*

Queen Connie looks fierce, but in reality, gorillas are generally calm and nonaggressive animals.

31

PURPLE MARTIN CAPITAL OF THE U.S.

WHAT: BIRDHOUSE-CRAZED TOWN
WHERE: GRIGGSVILLE, ILLINOIS, U.S.A.
Birdhouses might outnumber people houses in this small town. Nearly 5,000 bird condos line the town's main street, which has been renamed "Purple Martin Boulevard." It all started when rumors spread that these birds love to eat pesky mosquitoes, so the town's residents began building birdhouses to reduce the buzzing insect's numbers. One 40-foot (12-m) tower on Purple Martin Boulevard houses more than 600 birds. You could call it the Empire State Birding.

One purple martin may eat as many as 2,000 mosquitoes a day.

32

WEE'L TURTLE

WHAT: TIRE-RIM REPTILE
WHERE: DUNSEITH, NORTH DAKOTA, U.S.A.

Talk about coming out of your shell. Created from 2,000 tire rims, Wee'l Turtle is 40 feet (12 m) tall and bobs its head from side to side. Ten points if you can guess the name of the nearby mountains. (If you said "Turtle Mountains," you're a genius!)

BIRDHOUSE PARADISE

WHAT: BIRDHOUSE AND FLOWER BONANZA
WHERE: LOOGOOTEE, INDIANA, U.S.A.

This backyard is bursting with birdhouses! Homeowner Steve Larkin has quite the collection of brightly painted homes for his feathered friends—some 3,500 in all. But that's not all that attracts birds to this spot: Larkin also plants thousands of flowers for the fliers to feast on. Seeking a souvenir? Each guest walks away with a free birdhouse to take home. Bonus!

There are also dozens of dog statues found throughout Larkin's yard.

33

TOWN BUILT INTO ROCK

WHAT: LIVE BENEATH A BOULDER
WHERE: SETENIL DE LAS BODEGAS, SPAIN

Residents of this Spanish town are literally living under a rock! A massive rock formation sits atop shops, restaurants, and homes, giving the alarming appearance that they're about to be smashed. But people have lived beneath the rock, an overhang formed by a river flowing through town, for a long time. Someone figured out that if you add an exterior wall to the formation, voilà: You've got yourself a cool, cave-like casa! Today, tourists with their heads tilted up stroll the town's streets.

CREEPY GOLLUM

Japanese artist Masayuki Ohashi built the creepy 2,600-pound (1,200-kg) Gollum using epoxy resin, chainsaws, and robotics.

WHAT: HOBBIT HANGING AROUND
WHERE: WELLINGTON, NEW ZEALAND

A giant, hairy humanoid hand reaches out over your head while you wait for your bags at the Wellington International Airport. If you're a fan of the *Lord of the Rings* trilogy, you might find this 43-foot (13.1-m) flying hobbit sculpture more lovable than freakish. Installed in 2012 to celebrate the release of the first Hobbit movie, Gollum is still hanging around to welcome weary travelers to kiwi country.

FRESH WATER FISHING HALL OF FAME AND MUSEUM

Gone fishin'! This museum is only open from April through October.

WHAT: FISHING FOR FUN
WHERE: HAYWARD, WISCONSIN, U.S.A.

First things first: Climb into the mouth of the four-plus-stories-high leaping fish on the museum grounds. Then look out over Lake Hayward and plot the rest of your visit. Be sure to see the 300 mounted fish, including some world record holders, on display. And learn all about how to reel in the big ones before hitting the road again and trying your luck at one of the lakes riddling the region.

SAM HILL'S STONEHENGE

WHAT: STONEHENGE IN THE STATES
WHERE: MARYHILL, WASHINGTON, U.S.A.

Some might say Sam Hill's Stonehenge is a misunderstanding of monumental proportions. The full-scale replica of the famous prehistoric monument in England was built by a museum founder who mistakenly thought that the original Stonehenge was a monument to human sacrifice. (Many experts believe it was built to track the sun's movement.) He intended his Stonehenge to be a memorial to locals who had lost their lives in World War I. Despite the error, his monument is still an impressive imitation of the real deal, as well as a touching tribute.

Completed in 1929, the Stonehenge in Maryhill was the first World War I memorial in the United States.

CARHENGE

It took a team of around 30 people several weeks to build Carhenge.

WHAT: MONUMENT MADE OF CARS
WHERE: ALLIANCE, NEBRASKA, U.S.A.

You've heard of Stonehenge. But what about Carhenge? In the northwest corner of Nebraska, 39 automobiles stand on end and atop each other to mimic the mysterious English monument. Spray-painted gray to resemble the giant stones, the cars and trucks form a circle 96 feet (29 m) in diameter. The replica has a sweet story behind it: It was built in 1987 as a memorial to the artist's father, who once lived on the site.

DRAGON HEDGE

LAWN ON ROOF

WHAT: GRASS-COVERED ROOFS
WHERE: TÓRSHAVN, FAROE ISLANDS
Looks like lawn mowers have some new turf. On a group of islands near Iceland, roofs are covered in grass to trap heat and make homes warm throughout the year. To keep roofs from becoming jungles, workers must mow around buildings *and* on top of them. Still, chores are always more fun when they come with a view.

WHAT: MONSTROUS SHRUB
WHERE: EAST RUDHAM, NORFOLK, ENGLAND, U.K.

For the past 13 years, a man in England has sculpted his 150-foot (45.7-m)-long hedge into a giant green dragon. It started with a few arches to tame the wild bushes, and then the 10-foot (3-m)-high scaly creature was born, complete with wings, bulging eyes, flaring nostrils, a long tail, and a devilish smile. How does the sculptor keep this magical monster in check? Four electric hedge trimmers, two tall stepladders, and a lot of elbow grease.

The hedge has to be trimmed every two or three weeks.

BEN & JERRY'S FLAVOR GRAVEYARD

This is Nuts

The name was meant to say it all Without the pompous prose Was it nuts we chose to say so, or was it the nuts we chose?

2001-2002

WHAT: ICE-CREAM FLAVOR CEMETERY
WHERE: WATERBURY, VERMONT, U.S.A.

Holy cannoli! Ice-cream gurus Ben Cohen and Jerry Greenfield have been dreaming up delicious ice-cream flavors since 1978. While most of their flavors earn rave reviews, some do die along the way. So the company's owners created a cemetery along Vermont's scenic Route 100, complete with somber gray headstones, where their dearly de-pinted flavors can be savored for all eternity.

In 1983, Ben & Jerry's ice cream was used to make a supersize sundae in Vermont that tipped the scales at 27,102 pounds (12,293.3 kg).

SIDESPLITTING SHINDIGS

Whether it's wild races or curious parades, these eccentric events are worth a trip. Which one's the wackiest? You decide!

EUROPEAN BEARD CHAMPIONSHIPS

WHAT: BEARD VS. BEARD
WHERE: LEOGANG, AUSTRIA

Talk about a manly competition. More than 150 well-groomed gentlemen participate in the contest, which includes 17 categories—and a lot of hair spray. Contestants spruce up their facial art with curling irons, blow dryers, and sculpting wax. Clippers are *not* welcome.

Mustache categories include freestyle, Dali, and Musketeer.

GUANAJUATO INTERNATIONAL AIR BALLOON FESTIVAL

WHAT: FESTIVAL IN THE SKY
WHERE: LEÓN, MEXICO

This might be Princess Leia's worst nightmare. Participants at this festival soar across the sky in giant hot air balloons, such as this one shaped like Darth Vader's mask. More than 100 balloons fly each year—anything from pandas to bees to scarecrows. But don't worry. This Vader's only full of hot air.

A world record was set when 433 hot air balloons once soared simultaneously over France.

MEXICO CITY'S SUMMER CELEBRATION

WHAT: KERMIT SALUTES STATUE
WHERE: MEXICO CITY, MEXICO

It's easy being green when you're the star of the parade. A giant Kermit the Frog balloon floated by the capital's famous Angel of Independence monument as part of a parade to welcome summer. The Muppet was joined by the likes of Mickey Mouse and Spider-Man. Who knew frogs could fly?

OUTHOUSE RACE

WHAT: SKIING TOILET
WHERE: ANCHORAGE, ALASKA, U.S.A.

This event brings new meaning to "potty training." Alaska's most populous city hosts a winter festival each year to celebrate the state's history. A crowd favorite is the outhouse race, in which residents paint outhouses, or outdoor bathrooms, before pushing them through town on skis. Wonder if the prize is a golden plunger?

Aside from being the fastest, competitors can also pick up prizes for having the cleanest and most realistic-looking loos.

INTERNATIONAL PILLOW FIGHT DAY

WHAT: ATTACK OF THE FEATHERS
WHERE: BUDAPEST, HUNGARY

Feathers fly as a massive crowd bops each other with pillows. More than 100 cities participate in the April event, held to encourage people to get off their rumps and play.

Down pillows are discouraged in some cities because they make too much of a mess.

43

CORSO ZUNDERT

WHAT: FLOWERS ON PARADE
WHERE: ZUNDERT, NETHERLANDS

What's that smell? Flowers—lots of them. Every year, some 50,000 people head to this Dutch town to see an elaborate parade of petals. In addition to giraffes and other animals, the floats are shaped like giant monsters, cityscapes, motorcycles, ships, and yes, even flowers. Best-smelling parade ever.

Each float is made of wire, cardboard, and papier-mâché— then covered in thousands of flowers.

FLOWER FESTIVAL AND CAR PARADE

WHAT: PIG ON WHEELS
WHERE: MEDELLÍN, COLOMBIA

Oink, oink—er, *honk, honk!* Better get out of the way of this racing pig. The homemade car was one of many wacky vehicles that has taken part in a car parade that is part of Medellín's flower festival. This celebration is steeped in tradition and goes on for ten days. Wonder what other fun farm animals this swine swooped past?

ROYAL ASCOT

WHAT: ENGLISH BREAKFAST HAT
WHERE: ASCOT, ENGLAND, U.K.

Some people wear their pride on their sleeve—this fashionable woman wears hers on her hat. British patriotism is big at the Royal Ascot, an English horse race held every June. Among the hats worn by the crowd was this English breakfast: bacon, sausages, tomatoes, eggs, mushrooms, and beans. Wonder if she's willing to share.

Some 300,000 spectators, including the Queen of England, attend the Royal Ascot every year.

45

TIGER AND

The Tiger and Turtle is made of steel repurposed from a local mine.

IT LIGHTS UP!

TURTLE—
MAGIC MOUNTAIN

WHAT: WALK AND ROLL
WHERE: DUISBURG, GERMANY

From a distance, this steel sculpture might look like a far-out monster roller coaster, but you'll have to get out and stretch your legs to make it to the top. The Tiger and Turtle—Magic Mountain is actually a spiral staircase featuring a long narrow "track" made up of 249 steps complete with curves, dips, drops, and turns that take you as high as six stories above ground. Just don't try to walk those upside-down loops: They're just there for show.

DESTINATIONS FOR

DINOSAUR TRACKS

WHAT: FOSSILIZED FOOTSTEPS
WHERE: TUBA CITY, ARIZONA, U.S.A.
You can literally follow in the footsteps of giants at this dino-mite stop just east of the Grand Canyon. The series of footprints were left in wet earth nearly 200 million years ago by meat-eating *Dilophosaurus*. Fossilized over time, the three-lobed formations are a little longer than visitors' feet. After the turnoff, look for a guide to greet you and take you to the tracks, which are located on Navajo Nation land.

A series of fossilized footprints is called a trackway.

CABAZON DINOSAURS

WHAT: DINOS IN THE DESERT
WHERE: CABAZON, CALIFORNIA, U.S.A.
Your eyes don't deceive you: Those are giant dinosaurs standing in the California desert. The concrete *Apatosaurus* and *T. rex* have towered over the landscape for decades, drawing millions of tourists and making appearances in music videos, movies, and commercials. Stop in the shop in the belly of the 150-foot (46-m)-long *Apatosaurus* and then climb to the top of the *T. rex* to peer out from between its teeth for a dino's-eye view!

DINOSAUR DEVOTEES

If your rear end is Stego-sore-us from sitting in the car too long, ask your parents to pull over for a visit to one of these famous fossil stops.

GALLERIES OF PALEONTOLOGY AND COMPARATIVE ANATOMY

WHAT: A BONY MUSEUM EXHIBIT
WHERE: PARIS, FRANCE
No bones about it, this exhibit at the Muséum national d'histoire naturelle in Paris has a lot of skeletons in its closets. From the skeletal remains of whales and mastodon to hedgehogs, fish, and birds, visitors can observe and learn about the wonderful world of bones. You can even see the bones of animals like the extinct Steller's sea cow and fossils of dinosaurs like *Diplodocus*. Just one rule: Please don't feed the animals.

This exhibit features a "Cabinet of Curiosity," where visitors can check out preserved animal organs.

PARIS SEWER MUSEUM

WHAT: A DRAINING TOUR
WHERE: PARIS, FRANCE

Your trip through Paris will go right down the drain if you miss this underground 19th-century sewer tour. The entrance is located in the park just outside the Musée d'Orsay, on the city's Left Bank. Down below, you'll learn the history of the city's sewer system, its amazing engineering, the giant balls used to clean the tunnels, and the inner workings of a five-ton (4.5-t) "flushing boat." Think all that will make you, well, pooped? Don't worry, the tour only lasts an hour.

> The Paris sewer system is made up of 1,500 miles (2,400 km) of tunnels.

DENNIS SEVERS' HOUSE

WHAT: SPOOKY HOUSE
WHERE: LONDON, ENGLAND, U.K.

Dennis Severs was an artist who wanted his guests to feel as if they were part of a painting of what life used to be like within the walls of his historic home. And to this day, visitors take a step back in time—all the way to the early 18th century, when the house was built—once they enter this "living museum" at 18 Folgate Street. Stroll through the house and you'll get the sense that its occupants are still living there. But you're not being rude. Feeling like you're there is the whole idea. Was that a whisper coming from the next room? Hello? Is anybody home?

> Shhh! All tours through the Dennis Severs' House are conducted in complete silence.

GIANT PAUL BUNYAN AND BABE THE BLUE OX

WHAT: LARGER-THAN-LIFE STATUES
WHERE: BEMIDJI, MINNESOTA, U.S.A.

The statues are huge—and that's no tall tale! Giant replicas of the legendary lumberjack and his faithful friend Babe the Blue Ox welcome visitors in a major way. Living up to his larger-than-life legacy of lumberjacking, this folk hero replica is nearly as tall as a two-story building. And standing next to him is Babe. The pair have been on the National Register of Historic Places since 1988.

Babe's eyes glow with the help of battery-operated car lights.

BEMIDJI

PAUL

BUNYAN

1937

KOOKY COLLECTIONS

When someone takes the time to amass an amazing amount of items, you've got to stop and see what the obsession is all about.

SALT AND PEPPER SHAKER MUSEUM

The owners opened a sister museum in El Castell de Guadalest, Spain, that houses more than 20,000 pairs of shakers.

WHAT: CELEBRATING A CLASSIC COMBO
WHERE: GATLINBURG, TENNESSEE, U.S.A.

Salt and pepper—the two spices have been coupled for centuries, and this museum wasn't about to separate them. Stocked with more than 20,000 creative and kooky pairs of shakers from the 1500s to today, it's a popular stop for people en route to Great Smoky Mountains National Park. While you wander, learn fun facts, including the answer to the museum's most asked question: Which type of shaker—salt or pepper—has more holes? If you just can't shake the urge to buy your own set after your visit, keep in mind that the cost of admission goes toward a purchase from the gift shop.

PEZ

ORIGINAL PEZ
NEON SIGN

THIS SIGN HAS BEEN HANGING
ON THE PEZ HAAS-HOUSE
IN VIENNA, AUSTRIA
SINCE THE 1950'S
ARRIVED IN BURLINGAME
ON MAY 1, 2002

Licorice,
coffee, and
chlorophyll are all
former PEZ flavors.
No surprise they
aren't still
around!

BURLINGAME MUSEUM OF PEZ MEMORABILIA

WHAT: MUSEUM PACKED WITH PEZ HEADS
WHERE: BURLINGAME, CALIFORNIA, U.S.A.

At this sweet museum, peruse the 900-plus types of PEZ dispensers produced
since 1948. The cool candy containers are topped with everything from U.S.
presidents to Angry Birds characters, and many have become collectors' items.
The museum itself started as the owners' personal PEZ collection set up in
their computer shop. Today, the computers are gone, but there's a curator to
answer questions and a gift shop where visitors can purchase PEZ dispensers.

DOG COLLAR MUSEUM

WHAT: COLLECTION OF CANINE COLLARS
WHERE: KENT, ENGLAND, U.K.

This museum has gone to the dogs' ... collars, that is. Although its focus may seem strangely specific, its location may be even odder: within the walls of England's Leeds Castle. That's right: You can peruse a collection of more than 100 dog collars from five centuries and tour a medieval castle complete with a moat, all in one stop! The collars range from spiked, iron ones worn by hunting hounds to 21st-century chic neckwear for pampered pooches. All are a nod to the castle dwellers' long history of canine companions.

SHIN-YOKOHAMA RAMEN MUSEUM

WHAT: NOODLIN' AROUND
WHERE: YOKOHAMA, JAPAN

Slurp up some fun at a museum dedicated to the beloved noodle dish. Popular in Japan for more than half a century, ramen today comes in different styles specific to the country's regions. Taste them all at the museum's nine restaurants, decide which you like best, and then purchase as many packets as you like to take home. In between bites, watch how the noodles are made and read about their history while you stroll sets made to mimic a 1950s Tokyo neighborhood.

UNCLAIMED
BAGGAGE CENTER

WHAT: LOST AND FOUND EXTRAVAGANZA
WHERE: SCOTTSBORO, ALABAMA, U.S.A.

You never know what lost-luggage loot you'll find at this place, which sells stuff from unclaimed baggage lost during air travel. Shrewd shoppers scour the center's well-organized shelves to find all kinds of things, from wedding dresses and expensive watches to moose antlers, house slippers, and freeze-dried frogs. The center made a deal with major airlines: if it's not claimed, we'll buy it. They fill trucks with lost luggage and haul it to Alabama, where they stock the center's shelves. If you take off now, you might make it before closing time!

Airlines lose about 70,000 bags a year, which is actually less than one percent of all the luggage they carry.

Unclaimed Baggage® CENTER

INTERNATIONAL CRYPTOZOOLOGY MUSEUM

WHAT: A STUDY OF STRANGE ANIMALS
WHERE: PORTLAND, MAINE, U.S.A.

Bigfoot, Yeti, the Loch Ness Monster: Are these creatures real or fake? This one-of-a-kind collection showcases hair samples, footprints, and even waste said to be from various creatures most scientists say aren't real. But some people do believe, and this museum aims to make the case for why. Decide for yourself while wandering among eerie replicas, including an eight-foot (2.4-m) Bigfoot. You can also explore exhibits about animals verified by science only relatively recently, such as the okapi and the coelacanth. (Closed Tuesdays.)

The legend of the Loch Ness Monster is more than 1,500 years old!

Hot dog! The founder of the National Mustard Museum is known as the "Chief Mustard Officer."

America's Favorite Mustard

French's

Classic Yellow

· CHOLESTEROL FREE · 100% NATURAL · LOW IN FAT

THE NATIONAL MUSTARD MUSEUM

WHAT: MUSTARD-LOVERS' PARADISE
WHERE: MIDDLETON, WISCONSIN, U.S.A.

This place really cuts the mustard! The shrine to all things mustard in Dane County, Wisconsin, showcases more than 5,500 varieties of the yellow stuff. You can taste samples, read about the history of mustard, and even sing along with museum staff about the sometimes-spicy, sometimes-sweet spread. And for the love of mustard, while you're there, never, ever ask for ketchup!

SOUTH OF THE BORDER

WHAT: MASSIVE HIGHWAY REST STOP
WHERE: HAMER, SOUTH CAROLINA, U.S.A.

At 97 feet (29.6 m) tall and covered in lights, Pedro might just be the brightest guy around. He welcomes weary travelers just south of the state line between North Carolina and South Carolina, inviting them in for a place to sleep and eat, a carousel, an arcade, mini-golf, and even a reptile lagoon. Hey, Mom and Dad, are we there yet?

Nearly 200 highway billboards invite drivers from all directions to stop in at South of the Border.

KETCHUP BOTTLE WATER TOWER

WHAT: BIG KETCHUP BOTTLE
WHERE: COLLINSVILLE, ILLINOIS, U.S.A.

This bottle used to hold water, not ketchup. Built as a water tower for a ketchup factory, the structure is now a city landmark and holds, well, nothing. The 70-foot (21.3-m) ketchup bottle stands on 100-foot (30.5-m)-tall legs. Its cap is so big that a very tall man could lie down in it.

In Metropolis, you can visit the phone booth where the fictional character Clark Kent changed into his Superman suit.

OFFICIAL HOMETOWN OF SUPERMAN

WHAT: A HERO'S NATURAL HABITAT
WHERE: METROPOLIS, ILLINOIS, U.S.A.

It's not a bird, it's not a plane ... it's a supersize superhero in blue, standing in the center of downtown Metropolis. Right off exit 37 on Illinois Interstate 24, this is known as the Official Hometown of Superman. When you've had your fill of super-selfies, stroll down to the Super Museum and get a cape for the road. If you're lucky, you'll pass through the Man of Steel's hometown during the annual summer Superman Celebration.

TRUTH – JUSTICE – THE AMERICAN WAY

INSECTROPOLIS

Does it bug an insect to be touched? Not the fuzzy tarantula or the hissing cockroach at this creeping, crawling hands-on "bugseum." Yes, you can actually touch a live tarantula or a hissing cockroach (or a social scorpion or the merry millipede, if you prefer). This place is a friendly swarm of beautiful insects from bees to butterflies to beetles—and that's gnat a lie!

Male Madagascar hissing cockroaches sport large horns and can be up to three inches (7.5 cm) long.

PIANO AND VIOLIN HOUSE

WHAT: **IN-TUNE TOURIST STOP**
WHERE: **HUAINAN, CHINA**

Music lovers take note: Check out this crazy-cool structure shaped like massive musical instruments! An escalator inside a giant glass violin leads visitors to a black-and-white elevated building that resembles a grand piano. The propped-open "lid" of the piano is actually a covered terrace on the roof. Built in 2007 by nearby university students, the house isn't actually anyone's home but still attracts tourists to the region.

In 2014, China's president said in a speech that no more strange-looking structures should be built in the country's capital, Beijing.

OLD CAR CITY

WHAT: GIANT JUNKYARD FOR CLASSIC CARS
WHERE: WHITE, GEORGIA, U.S.A.

Here's a place where vintage vehicles go to *rust* in peace. Stroll the grounds of this giant junkyard and check out more than 4,000 classic cars scattered throughout the woods. And because most of the vehicles haven't been moved in decades, they've literally become one with nature: Plymouths poke out from thick groves of trees, while weeds wrap around rusty Fords. Look closely and you may see an old pickup under a pile of pine needles. Sure puts a new spin on going green! (Closed Sunday–Tuesday.)

Old Car City's collection features cars all built before 1972.

WHAT: A-MAZING JUNGLE OF CORN
WHERE: CHESTER, NEW JERSEY, U.S.A

Every year, Stony Hill Farm Market picks a sweet theme for its awesome ten-acre (4-ha) corn maze, like trains, pirates, or pyramids that puzzle, confuse, and bewilder visitors to this destination. If you're really brave, stalk through the eerie maze at night, armed only with a flashlight.

Native Americans chewed the leaves of sweet corn stalks like chewing gum.

In 2015, the corn palace underwent a huge corn-struction project to renovate.

CORN PALACE

WHAT: CASTLE DE CORN
WHERE: MITCHELL, SOUTH DAKOTA, U.S.A.

Don't miss this ear-resistible place as you're road-tripping through South Dakota. Every year the corny Main Street attraction gets decorated inside and out with "crop art," that is, colorful murals made from 12 varieties of corn. Stop by for a free tour of this a-maize-ing place, or drive through in August for the annual corn festival.

MOST PECULIAR PLACES

Think you've seen it all? Think again: These stops are so weird, they're sure to surprise even the most seasoned road travelers.

MYSTERY SPOT

WHAT: GRAVITY GOES WILD
WHERE: SANTA CRUZ, CALIFORNIA, U.S.A.

The attraction's name alone leaves passersby wondering: What in the world is it, anyway? Without giving away the answer, here are a few hints: The sights you see in this building may make you think up is down and down is up, may make you fall over, and may even make you a little queasy! The spot's website says only that it's a "gravitational anomaly located in the redwoods" 150 feet (46 m) in diameter. Wait times for the 45-minute tour can be long, but nearby hiking trails help keep visitors entertained.

Oregon, Michigan, and West Virginia are also home to "mystery spots."

GOATS ON THE ROOF

WHAT: GOATS GO UPSTAIRS TO GRAZE
WHERE: TIGER, GEORGIA, U.S.A.

You've heard of ants on a log. But what about goats on a roof? That's exactly what you'll see at this roadside store that claims its animals like to climb up top because they're direct descendants of aliens. Roast marshmallows, play arcade games and air hockey, and snack on fudge and ice cream while you watch the goats frolic on the fenced-in rooftop. You can even send up a bucket full of food to them!

HOMEMADE
ICE CREAM FUDGE

HOME
FUDGE
ICE CREAM

BIG BILLY'S
CAFE & SWEET TREATS

The shop's owners entice the goats to climb onto the roof by keeping plenty of food to graze on up there.

PIKE PLACE MARKET GUM WALL

WHAT: GROSS GUM GATHERING
WHERE: SEATTLE, WASHINGTON, U.S.A.

Need to get rid of your gum? Ditch it on this icky, sticky wall at Seattle's famous Pike Place Market. A colorful coating of the chewy candy covers a stretch of brick wall and even oozes off windowsills along the otherwise pretty Post Alley. People waiting in line for the theater first added their wads to the wall in the 1990s. Now the site is a top spot for tourists to take a photo and leave their mark. As of 2015, officials plan to pressure wash the roughly 20 years' worth of wads (more than six inches [15 cm] thick in some spots!). But never fear—they fully expect this will create a clean canvas for fresh globs of gooey gum.

While you're on the West Coast, see if you can also add a wad to the walls of Bubblegum Alley in San Luis Obispo, California.

FREMONT TROLL

WHAT: MONSTER BENEATH A BRIDGE
WHERE: SEATTLE, WASHINGTON, U.S.A.

Feeling brave? Climb onto a giant troll clutching a Volkswagen Beetle in the funky Seattle neighborhood of Fremont! Built by local artists in 1990, this creepy concrete creature appears to be crawling out of a hiding spot beneath a bridge, and it peers at passersby with a single, shiny eye—a hubcap. Every year, costumed revelers gather at the troll to celebrate its birthday: Halloween, of course!

Up for more spooky spots in Seattle? On the Underground Tour, explore city blocks destroyed in an 1889 fire that today lie beneath downtown streets.

The general store that used to be attached to the two-story outhouse was torn down in 1984.

1022

TWO-STORY OUTHOUSE

WHAT: DOUBLE-DECKER TOILETS

WHERE: GAYS, ILLINOIS, U.S.A.

It's a curious sight on the side of the road: a double-decker outhouse that might leave you wondering how someone using the lower level could avoid things falling from above. Not to worry: The upper "throne" of this historic attraction from the 1800s (it once connected to a second-floor apartment above a general store), has holes set back and a false wall to prevent accidents below. What a relief!

DURAVIT DESIGN CENTER'S EXTRA-LARGE LOO

WHAT: GIANT TOILET
WHERE: HORNBERG, GERMANY

Just south of Gutach off Germany's highway B33, this bathroom design center houses the biggest toilet you've ever seen. This larger-than-life lavatory serves as an observation deck—no potty-talk allowed! From the top (it's about three stories high), you'll see a flush view of Germany's famous Black Forest. But if peeing is what you need to do, don't throw your plans down the toilet. The building has plenty of working bathrooms.

> Around the world, toilets are also known as "loos," "latrines," and "privies."

LEILA'S HAIR MUSEUM

WHAT: SHRINE TO HUMAN HAIR
WHERE: INDEPENDENCE, MISSOURI, U.S.A.

Here's a hair-raising fact: Art made with human hair can be traced back as far as the 12th century. This modern-day museum keeps up the tradition by making hair its "mane" attraction. You don't want to miss the opportunity to stop and browse thousands of artifacts—from bracelets to bookmarks, buttons, and beautiful wreaths—all made of hair.

> The museum features locks of hair belonging to such celebrities as Michael Jackson and Marilyn Monroe.

KERET HOUSE

WHAT: WORLD'S NARROWEST HOUSE
WHERE: WARSAW, POLAND

Talk about close quarters! Just 48 inches (122 cm) across at its widest point, 28 inches (71 cm) at its narrowest, Keret House, incredibly, is home sweet home for someone! Israeli short-story writer Etgar Keret first stayed there, and now other artists reside in shifts. The home's shiny, skinny exterior can be hard to spot: It's wedged in an alley in Warsaw's Wola district. On select days each month, visitors can step inside for a (tiny) tour.

MUSEUM OF BAD ART

WHAT: CELEBRATION OF ARTISTIC BLOOPERS
WHERE: SOMERVILLE, MASSACHUSETTS, U.S.A.

This funky museum celebrates masterpiece mistakes, like a portrait in which the subject of the painting (accidentally) looks like the man is sitting on a toilet. Or the painting resulting from an experiment in color technique gone wrong, in which the people appear more Easter egg than human. The collection includes about 250 beautiful blunders, some of which are on display outside the men's room of a movie theater.

Welcome TO NORTH POLE ALASKA

THE HOME OF SANTA CLAUS

...Where dreams come true...

SANTA CLAUS HOUSE

WHAT: WHERE SANTA LIVES
WHERE: NORTH POLE, ALASKA, U.S.A.

Dashing through this small town, you might run into a few old friends, like a giant statue of St. Nick that sits outside the Santa Claus House on the side of Richardson Highway. Take off your coat and stay for a while: The jolly man has been waiting all year to see you. Have your picture taken with a cheerful reindeer, browse the gift shop, and sip a cup of cocoa—at this merry place, it's Christmas every day.

Visitors are welcomed by a giant Santa Claus, measuring taller than a giraffe!

LONDON BRIDGE IN AZ

WHAT: BRIDGE TRANSPLANT
WHERE: LAKE HAVASU, ARIZONA, U.S.A.

In the famous nursery rhyme, London Bridge is falling down. But not to worry, somebody rebuilt the famous, nearly 200-year-old trestle 5,200 miles (8,369 km) away in Arizona. Pieces were dismantled, numbered, and shipped all the way to the United States. It reopened in 1971. These days, you can drive over it, walk over it, tour it, and even buy a chip of it to take home. As for the antique lamps positioned on the side of the bridge? They were made of melted war cannons from the 1800s. What a blast!

The bridge is said to be haunted by a British police officer who patrols at night.

DINNER IN THE SKY

The world's highest restaurant is inside the Burj Khalifa in Dubai—set at a lofty 1,350 feet (422 m) aboveground.

WHAT: SKY-HIGH RESTAURANT
WHERE: BRUSSELS, BELGIUM

Whatever you do, don't drop your silverware. Dinner in the Sky lifts its diners, table, and waitstaff about 160 feet (49 m) into the air for a meal. Guests are strapped to their seats the entire time. Although this one is based in Belgium, the restaurant can be driven almost anywhere. Next stop, space?

ICE-COVERED LIGHTHOUSE

WHAT: LIGHTHOUSE BECOMES ICICLE
WHERE: ST. JOSEPH, MICHIGAN, U.S.A.

Add a little cherry flavoring and this thing would've been perfect on a summer day. If you happen to be driving around Lake Michigan after a winter storm, be sure to stop and take a look at this lighthouse. In 2015, strong winds blew waves and mist onto the St. Joseph lighthouse and they froze, coating it with layers of ice. Too bad no one could enter this in an ice sculpture contest.

WORLD'S DEEPEST
UNDERWATER MAILBOX

郵便
POST

WHAT: MAIL GOES SWIMMING
WHERE: SUSAMI BAY, JAPAN

Collecting letters from this mailbox requires more than a
mailbag—you need a wet suit and an air tank. Located about
33 feet (10 m) beneath the sea, the underwater mail drop
can hold about 200 waterproof postcards sent by divers.
We hope sharks never come looking for a food delivery.

ELECTRIC LADYLAND

WHAT: MUSEUM OF FLUORESCENT ART
WHERE: AMSTERDAM, NETHERLANDS

You'll light up when you visit this place—literally! This small basement museum celebrates a blinding love of fluorescent light. Downstairs in this row house on a narrow, bicycle-lined Amsterdam street, you'll see the light in artwork, stones, crystals, and minerals that sparkle and shine. You'll even start to glow as you become part of the interactive exhibit.

Some minerals, like calcite, tremolite and fluorite, glow under ultraviolet light.

FRED SMITH'S WISCONSIN CONCRETE PARK

WHAT: ROCK-SOLID SCULPTURES
WHERE: PHILLIPS, WISCONSIN, U.S.A.

Fred Smith was a folk artist on a mission. During his life, he created hundreds of concrete sculptures of things he admired, from moose to mules, muscled workhorses to world leaders. Today, his sculptures are scattered throughout this park for future generations to enjoy. You could say this artist's legacy is set in stone.

Fred Smith's sculptures are decorated with recycled materials like glass bottles, car parts, and mirrors.

SPOOKY SITES

You might hit the road running after being scared silly at one of these delightfully daunting destinations. Do you dare?

CATACOMBS OF PARIS

WHAT: AN EERIE UNDERGROUND CEMETERY
WHERE: PARIS, FRANCE

Descend 130 steps and enter a dark, chilly maze stretching 1.2 miles (2 km) beneath the streets of Paris, also known as the city's famous catacombs. Some six million Parisian skeletons were relocated from city cemeteries in the 17th and 18th centuries to this underground space after it was deemed more sanitary for the living. A 45-minute tour walks you through tunnels lined with bones and gives you a glimpse of Paris's past—the catacombs once held stone that workers removed to build the city above. (Closed Mondays.)

All bags are searched upon exiting the catacombs to ensure no one steals any bones!

NATIONAL MUSEUM OF FUNERAL HISTORY

WHAT: QUIRKY COFFINS ON DISPLAY
WHERE: HOUSTON, TEXAS, U.S.A.

Are you dying to check out this morbid museum? It offers a fascinating look at how humans handle the grim business of death, with everything from a coffin built of coins and dollar bills to items used in the funerals of popes and presidents. Exhibits also cover embalming—first practiced by the ancient Egyptians—and Dia de los Muertos, the holiday to celebrate the dead held in Mexico and elsewhere. Be sure to see the coffins from Ghana carved to look like everything from animals to airplanes.

The museum's slogan is "Any day above ground is a good one."

Bran castle was once home to Romania's royal family.

BRAN CASTLE

WHAT: HOME OF COUNT DRACULA
WHERE: TRANSYLVANIA, ROMANIA

If you happen to be driving from the Romanian city of Brasov to the nearby village of Bran, be sure to stop at the spooky, ancient castle jutting out of the rocks above. The mysterious castle was the inspiration for the home of Bram Stoker's legendary blood-sucking character, Dracula. The towering castle has about 60 rooms, many connected by narrow, winding staircases and underground passageways—and still filled with bearskin rugs and ancient weapons and armor. But don't get too excited: No members of the undead actually ever lived there (at least we don't think they did!).

77

MEDIEVAL CRIME MUSEUM

WHAT: HOUSE OF TORTURE
WHERE: ROTHENBURG OB DER TAUBER, GERMANY

Courts in the Middle Ages used torture to extract confessions or details of a crime, and to punish criminals. At the Medieval Crime Museum, you can find gruesome tools that squeezed fingers, crushed bones, and chopped body parts off criminals. Check out the baker's chair, once used to punish bakers caught selling customers smaller-than-average loaves of bread. Shackled into too-small metal chairs, the offending bakers were left on the street to be ridiculed and beaten—all in the name of the law.

Schandmaske
mit Schellen
Shame Mask
with bells

Spangenhaube 17./18. Jahrhundert
Bonnet with buckle 17/18th centuries

KUNSTKAMERA

WHAT: MONSTER MUSEUM
WHERE: ST. PETERSBURG, RUSSIA

Sightseeing in St. Petersburg? Don't miss this monstrous collection of strange stuff, like the skeleton of Siamese twins, preserved human tumors, and one stuffed pangolin, or scaly anteater. The unusual collection came together in the early 1700s as ruler Peter the Great collected and preserved bizarre specimens during his travels around the globe. It's all secreted away on the third floor of the Peter the Great Museum of Anthropology and Ethnography.

Peter the Great loved science and studied both the living and the dead.

OLD OPERATING THEATRE MUSEUM

WHAT: HISTORIC OPERATING ROOM
WHERE: LONDON, ENGLAND, U.K.

From the street, St. Thomas Church looks pretty ordinary. But back in the early 1800s, its attic—accessible only by a creaky, narrow spiral staircase—served as an operating room for the hospital next door. Today, reenactors in this upstairs medical museum demonstrate ghastly (and excruciating) 200-year-old traditions, some that involve grisly looking knives, needles, saws, hooks, and other scary old-fashioned surgical instruments. Watch out: This place will leave you in stitches.

Doctors used to cover the floor of the attic operating room with sawdust to keep blood from dripping into the church below.

EDINBURGH VAULTS

WHAT: CREEPY UNDERGROUND CHAMBERS
WHERE: EDINBURGH, SCOTLAND, U.K.

If these dark, scary walls could talk, they'd tell stories of misery, murder, and mayhem. The dark, dusty chambers (about 120 of them) underneath Edinburgh's arched South Bridge housed some of the area's poorest souls in the late 1700s. Some say whispering, chilling ghosts are the only inhabitants left of these cramped, damp, stuffy spaces full of doom. Tour the vaults ... if you dare!

Visitors have reported feeling the presence of a ghost child named Jack who's said to haunt the vaults.

You can also learn about ancient astronauts, crop circles, alien abductions, and other spine-tingling things at the museum.

INTERNATIONAL UFO MUSEUM AND RESEARCH CENTER

WHAT: ALL THINGS ALIEN
WHERE: ROSWELL, NEW MEXICO, U.S.A.

A mysterious incident occurred in the New Mexico desert during a thunderstorm the night of July 4, 1947. Was it a crash landing of a flying saucer, covered up by the U.S. government? Simply a weather balloon accident? Or something else? Explore all of these possibilities and more at this museum of out-of-this-world encounters. Displays include soil from the nearby mystery site. Visit during the first week of July and you can catch the annual Roswell UFO Festival, which includes a parade and costume contests for people and pets!

POPS

WHAT: GIANT SOFT DRINK BOTTLE
WHERE: ARCADIA, OKLAHOMA, U.S.A.

When you see that colorful soda bottle covered in bubbly lights on the side of Route 66, you'll know it's time for a pit stop. Watch for Pops just northeast of Oklahoma City, near a town called Edmond. The owner named his restaurant after his dad, and he celebrates their shared passion for road trips and carbonation with a sweet 66-foot (20-m) sculpture.

Pops stocks more than 600 fizzy flavors of soda for thirsty travelers, including Freaky Dog Watermelon, Rocket Fizz Mud Pie Soda, and Jones Fufu Berry.

BRAIN-SHAPED PHONE BOOTH

WHAT: PHONE GROWS BRAIN
WHERE: SÃO PAULO, BRAZIL

Need a little extra brainpower? This brain-shaped phone booth was part of a design competition. A hundred designs—including a disco ball, a ladybug, an ear, and a clown—were installed over public telephones in Brazil's largest city. Cell phones have never seemed so boring.

SUSPENDED WATER TAP

WHAT: WATER FAUCET FLOATS!
WHERE: YPRES, BELGIUM

What's the trick to this floating faucet? A clear pipe inside the falling water creates the illusion. The supportive pipe carries water from a pool on the ground to the rear of the faucet. The water loops around and is spewed back out into the pool. That's why it looks like an unending flow of water. Now we're thirsty.

"Floating" faucets can also be found in Canada, England, Spain, Switzerland, and the United States.

ENCHANTED HIGHWAY

WHAT: SCRAP-METAL SCULPTURES
WHERE: GLADSTONE, NORTH DAKOTA, U.S.A.

The 32-mile (51-km) stretch of road between Regent and Gladstone, North Dakota, is home to plenty of wildlife and farms. But you'll also spot a fisherman, hovering above the highway in a red boat hoping to hook a big fish, and a scrap-metal goose with a wingspan as long as a limo, among other colorful creations. A local artist sculpted seven of these eye-catching, monster-size art installments to turn this highway from lonesome to delightful.

SHOBAK CASTLE TUNNELS

WHAT: REMARKABLE RUINS
WHERE: ASH-SHIBEK, JORDAN

From the outside, Shobak Castle doesn't look like much. After all, the crumbling fortress was originally constructed on top of a hill in the 12th century and has been knocked down—and rebuilt—during different wars. But within those sun-scorched brick walls you'll find a fortress filled with tiny rooms and impressive archways still intact even after several earthquakes. Head down a secret tunnel cut into the rock and follow the slippery, sandy staircase all the way to an underground spring some 100 feet (30 m) down. Just be sure to bring a headlamp—and a heaping dose of courage: The narrow passageway is pitch dark!

BOXING CROCODILE

WHAT: CROCIN' SOCKIN'
WHERE: HUMPTY DOO, AUSTRALIA

This is one crocodile you needn't be afraid of. The 27-foot (8-m) Big Boxing Crocodile stands outside a gas station in an area called the Northern Territory, known for its large number of saltwater crocodiles. As to why this tourist-attracting croc is wearing boxing gloves ... your guess is as good as ours.

SHOP COVERED IN BICYCLES

WHAT: BIKES SCALE BUILDING
WHERE: ALTLANDSBERG, GERMANY

This bicycle store is totally off the wall. To advertise his goods, the owner mounted more than 120 bikes on the front of his four-story shop. The two-wheelers—attached to the building with metal brackets—are all different sizes, colors, and models. Good thing this guy doesn't own a car dealership.

Most of the mounted bikes are used trade-ins brought in by customers.

POLAR BEAR SWIM

WHAT: SHARK GETS FRIENDLY
WHERE: VANCOUVER, CANADA

One fake shark brings new meaning to the phrase "biting cold." Celebrating the new year, participants in this annual event wade into the chilly 44°F (6.7°C) waters of English Bay wearing kooky costumes—or just their bathing suits. The plunge also raises money for charity. No cold-hearted people here.

There's a similar sculpture by the same artist rising from the ground in Punta del Este, Uruguay.

HAND OF THE DESERT

WHAT: GIANT HAND SCULPTURE
WHERE: ATACAMA DESERT, CHILE

Not much grows in this desert. In fact, there are spots where rainfall has never been recorded. But *something* is sprouting—a giant hand that reaches out of the sand! Built to draw visitors to the nearby city of Antofagasta, the three-story Hand of the Desert is a cement sculpture with an iron base. It's strong enough to withstand both the blistering desert heat and freezing nighttime temperatures.

WACKIEST (NEARLY) NATURAL WONDERS

Mother Nature creates some of the best places in the world to pull over. See how humans have highlighted these awesome (almost) au naturel attractions.

It's said that Deer Cave's bats eat up to 30 tons (27 t) of mosquitoes every night.

DEER CAVE

WHAT: BAT CAVE WITH ABE LINCOLN'S PROFILE
WHERE: MIRI, SARAWAK, MALAYSIAN BORNEO

Holy Honest Abe, Batman! Take a look at the rock formations by Deer Cave's southern entrance and you'll be able to make out a perfect profile of President Abraham Lincoln—beard and all. At more than 1.2 miles (2 km) long and 571 feet (174 m) high, Deer Cave is one of the world's largest cave passages. Stick around at sunset and watch as a mega cloud of free-tailed bats emerges from the cave in search of food. Experts estimate the bats living here number in the billions—more than any other single cave on the planet.

ABE, IS THAT YOU?

METEOR CRATER VISITOR CENTER

WHAT: HUGE HOLE IN THE GROUND
WHERE: OUTSIDE WINSLOW, ARIZONA, U.S.A.
What's cooler than standing at the rim of a nearly one-mile (1.6-km)-wide crater created by a crash-landing meteorite 50,000 years ago? Not much! To get a sense of the crater's size, peer through a telescope and see if you can spot the 6-foot (2-m) astronaut cutout 570 feet (173 m) down at the bottom. Inside the visitor center, watch a movie that uses 3-D animation to re-create the awesome destruction of the ancient impact. On your way out, stop at the gift and rock shops for fossils, stone jewelry, quartz crystals, and petrified wood.

A fence keeps curious onlookers out of the crater. Well, most of the time: In 2013, a man jumped over and had to be rescued!

89

The tree gets its name from the shape of its broadly arching branches.

CHANDELIER TREE

Height: 315ft Diameter: 21ft
Maximum Age: 2400yrs
DRIVE THRU TREE, Leggett, CA

CHANDELIER TREE

WHAT: DRIVE-THRU TREE
WHERE: LEGGETT, CALIFORNIA, U.S.A.

Here's a roadside attraction you can enjoy without ever leaving the comfort of your car. Within the appropriately named Drive-Thru Tree Park lives the Chandelier Tree, a 315-foot (96-m)-tall behemoth that cars and motorcycles can roll right through. A giant hole was cut into the base of the 2,000-year-old tree in the 1930s to attract tourists to the area. It worked: The tree still draws lots of visitors, and the surrounding parkland includes a duck pond, picnic area, hiking trails, and a gift shop. Now if only you could purchase food from the tree while driving through it ...

MASAYA VOLCANO NATIONAL PARK

WHAT: TOUR AN ACTIVE VOLCANO
WHERE: OUTSIDE MANAGUA, NICARAGUA

A visit to this active Central American volcano is a blast—literally! Masaya regularly spews plumes of gas, and in 2012 there was even a series of ash and rock explosions! Just 16 miles (26 km) from Nicaragua's capital, the volcano offers lots of options for thrill-seekers, including trails to the edge of craters and a bat-filled cave. For those who aren't afraid of the dark, there's a night tour that winds its way through a tunnel and then to a viewpoint of distant glowing, red lava!

Packs of colorful parakeets live inside the volcano.

KASHA-KATUWE TENT ROCKS NATIONAL MONUMENT

WHAT: WEIRD-SHAPED ROCKS
WHERE: COCHITI PUEBLO, NEW MEXICO, U.S.A.

Given enough time, Mother Nature can do weird things with rock. Here, through the powerful forces of volcanism and erosion over more than a million years, rock has been shaped into odd-looking cones. The formations resemble a crowd of capped gnomes congregating in the desert—if gnomes could grow as tall as 90 feet (27 m)! Cool hiking trails winding between rocks take you to narrow slot canyons and sweeping lookouts. Be sure to look down while you roam: Fragments of obsidian, or volcanic glass, litter the ground.

It's against the law to take any volcanic glass home with you.

PETRIFIED FOREST NATIONAL PARK

WHAT: ANCIENT WOODS OF WONDER
WHERE: HOLBROOK, ARIZONA, U.S.A.

This detour-worthy stop will blow your mind with colorful fossil logs that are more than 200 million years old. Lace up your hiking boots and hit the dirt in one of the park's beautiful wilderness areas, filled with petrified wood—ancient wood that's turned into stone over time. There's nothing scary about the Petrified Forest, which stretches out over 135,000 ancient acres (54,633 ha). That is, unless you start thinking about the dinosaurs that once roamed the vast landscape.

It takes millions of years for wood to turn into quartz crystals.

BILLY TRIPP'S MINDFIELD

WHAT: A MINDFUL MASTERPIECE
WHERE: BROWNSVILLE, TENNESSEE, U.S.A.

Artist Billy Tripp speaks with his hands and a whole lot of scrap metal. If you're driving east of Memphis, you can see his massive sculpture on the right side of the road squeezed in behind a tiny motel. From a distance it might look like a tangle of metal, but look closer and you'll find words of inspiration and objects like hearts carved out of metal. Tripp started his work in 1989 and still keeps his pedal to the metal, working on the sculpture every day.

WIELICZKA SALT MINE

WHAT: A CELEBRATION OF SALT
WHERE: WIELICZKA, POLAND

Did you know that ancient Romans used salt like money? Miners harvested the valuable stuff from this place for more than 900 years. But they left something behind: treasures like an underground lake and a captivating cathedral complete with working chandeliers carved into the salt walls about 600 feet (183 m) below ground. Going down?

The rock salt found in the Wieliczka Salt Mine formed in the Earth more than 12 million years ago.

ESHIMA OHASHI BRIDGE

WHAT: MIND-BOGGLING BRIDGE
WHERE: MATSUE, JAPAN

The Eshima Ohashi bridge—which spans a mile (1.6 km) over Lake Nakaumi—looks more like a roller coaster than a road. Connecting two towns in southwest Japan, the bridge is built high enough to let ships pass underneath and stands some 14 stories (44 m) at its tallest point. Just make sure you're buckled in tight—navigating Eshima Ohashi's fairly steep descent is the stuff that'll make your stomach flip for sure.

The world's tallest bridge, France's Millau Viaduct, is taller than the Eiffel Tower.

The nighttime tour of the House on the Rock will rock your world with its haunted carousel and zombies.

HOUSE ON THE ROCK

WHAT: ROCKY RETREAT
WHERE: SPRING GREEN, WISCONSIN, U.S.A.

If you're traveling through southern Wisconsin and you find yourself between a rock and hard place, then you're just a stone's throw away from this awesome attraction. The rock-solid house was built in 1945 to take advantage of the beautiful views of the surrounding area. Since then, the place has been expanded to include an inn and a golf course, and bizarre exhibits, including collections of medieval armor, carousel horses, chandeliers, dolls, and cannons. You're off your rocker if you miss this place!

TOUR 3
CONTINU

BRADERIE DE LILLE

WHAT: QUIRKY OPEN-AIR MARKET
WHERE: LILLE, FRANCE

Ever seen a strolling great white? A shark-shaped headpiece is one of thousands of quirky purchases you can make at Braderie de Lille, or the street market of Lille. The event, Europe's biggest flea market, welcomes some two million visitors every September and dates back to the 12th century. The real sharks here are the bargain hunters.

GIANT EYEBALL
SCULPTURE

WHAT: EYEBALL SPIES ON CITY
WHERE: DALLAS, TEXAS, U.S.A.

You won't need binoculars to spot this giant eyeball on Main Street in Dallas. Made of steel and fiberglass, the art stands more than three stories (9.4 m) tall. Artist Tony Tasset modeled the sculpture after one of his own blue eyes. Bet this body part has caused some epic staring contests.

Before landing in Dallas, the eyeball had stints in Chicago, Illinois, and Sparta, Wisconsin.

ROADSIDE AMERICA MINIATURE VILLAGES

WHAT: TINY TOWNS
WHERE: SHARTLESVILLE, PENNSYLVANIA, U.S.A.

Just off Highway 78 in Pennsylvania's famous Dutch country, stop in for a little fun along the way. On display, you'll find miles of marvelously detailed mini-model villages, complete with homes, at least one circus, barns, an airport, street scenes, a coal mine, caves, waterfalls, and mountains. Each of the eight villages shows a different period of American history. If you're lucky, you'll get to see the sun set when the lighting goes down, the little lamps inside the buildings come on, and stars on the ceiling begin to twinkle.

There are more than 10,000 handmade trees in the mini villages' green forests.

CHEVROLET DEGLER CHEVROLET OLDSMOBILE
HAMBURG, PA.

98

BUND SIGHTSEEING TUNNEL

WHAT:
KALEIDOSCOPIC TOURIST RIDE
WHERE:
SHANGHAI, CHINA

Why use a bridge to cross a river when you can travel beneath it? An automated car moving through an underwater tunnel whisks you across the Huangpu River in this popular Shanghai tourist attraction. A bizarre, bright light show set to a strange soundtrack makes the ride a feast for the eyes and ears. Be sure not to blink: The total length of the tunnel is less than half a mile so it's over in less than five minutes.

The Bund ride can shuttle 5,280 passengers per hour.

TRAFFIC LIGHT TREE

WHAT: TREE STOPS TRAFFIC
WHERE: LONDON, ENGLAND, U.K.

Money doesn't grow on trees—but traffic lights might! This 26-foot (8-m)-high treelike structure is made of 75 sets of traffic lights controlled by computers. The sculpture, created by a French artist to represent the energy of the city around it, has been a big hit with locals. Sounds like this fake tree has really taken root.

The sculpture is as tall as some trees, but this tree won't be doing any growing.

RADICAL REPLICAS

You'll think you're seeing double when you tour these towns made to look and feel like famous cities—just a continent away!

PHONE

市政广场 中央休闲商业街
CITY HALL CENTRAL RECREATION & COMMERCIAL DISTRICT

THAMES TOWN · SONGJIANG

Thames Town is a popular spot for wedding photos.

THAMES TOWN

WHAT: ENGLISH CHARM IN CHINA
WHERE: OUTSIDE SHANGHAI, CHINA

Should you find yourself longing for London while staying in Shanghai, you're in luck. The suburb of Thames Town, named for the river that runs through London, looks remarkably like an English village but is just a few miles from the massive Chinese city. The copycat pulls off the feat with cobblestone streets, classic British building facades, red telephone booths, statues of famous Brits such as Harry Potter and Princess Diana, and even a (man-made) river streaming through it!

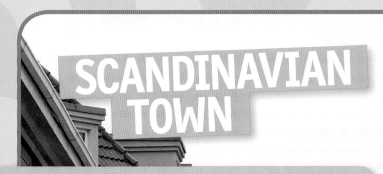

SCANDINAVIAN TOWN

WHAT: A SLICE OF SWEDEN IN SHANGHAI
WHERE: SHANGHAI, CHINA

Standing in the center of Luodian, a small city outside of Shanghai, you may not be able to tell whether you're in China or Sweden. With its red-roofed buildings, cobblestone streets, and European-inspired architecture, Luodian is a replica of a typical Swedish town. Stroll along the tree-lined canal or hop into a row boat and paddle around the man-made Lake Malaren just as you would in, say, Stockholm. But visit in June, and you'll get a definite Chinese vibe: The lake is home to an annual dragon boat festival, an ancient Chinese tradition dating back to the 14th century.

SKY CITY

The Eiffel Tower in Sky City is about a third of the size of the real deal in Paris.

WHAT: CITY OF LIGHT LOOK-ALIKE
WHERE: OUTSIDE HANGZHOU, CHINA

Is it possible to pull off visiting Paris without ever leaving China? You bet! Less than an hour's drive from Hangzhou, a sprawling metropolis of more than six million people, sits a replica of the famous French capital. It has Parisian-looking boulevards, balconies, fountains, and even a mini Eiffel Tower! Intended to be luxury residences, the buildings are largely empty, giving the city the feel of an eerily abandoned Paris.

VENICE WATER TOWN

WHAT: ITALIAN IMITATION
WHERE: OUTSIDE HANGZHOU, CHINA

Venice, Italy, is one of the most popular places to visit in the world. So it's no surprise it's one of China's more popular "replica cities." This re-creation comes complete with canals and other famous Venetian features, such as St. Mark's Square. Gondoliers navigate the faux Italian city's signature boats beneath stone bridges and between picturesque townhouses lining the waterways. See if you can spot some of the not-so-authentic touches, like the basketball court in St. Mark's Square.

SAN FRANCISCO'S CHINATOWN

WHAT: A SLICE OF CHINA IN CALIFORNIA
WHERE: SAN FRANCISCO, CALIFORNIA, U.S.A.

San Francisco's Chinatown neighborhood is so big and buzzing with activity that it feels more like a city within a city. On the map since the mid-1800s, a dozen or so square blocks became what's called the largest Chinatown outside Asia and the oldest in North America. A maze of shops full of fascinating goods, squeezed side by side with ornate, historic buildings, makes for a full day of exploration. Be sure to start at the official entrance, the Chinatown Gate, a three-tiered archway flanked by fearsome stone lions.

There are also Chinatowns in Havana, Cuba, Johannesburg, South Africa, and Melbourne, Australia, among other spots around the world.

WILD RIDES

WAGON TRAIN

Bob Castanada fondly remembers his childhood red wagon, so he built his own grown-up version. The plywood Radio Flyer is built on the frame of a hot rod racer. In winter, Castanada modifies the wagon to become Santa's sleigh—complete with a fake reindeer in the front.

Cross a regular four-wheeled vehicle with tons of imagination, and you might just get an art car. "When you see an art car, you're viewing someone's individuality," says art car builder Harrod Blank. Some can be driven on the streets; others are just for show. But all of them are head-turners. Check out these photos to see how car-tists express themselves on wheels.

QUILTING THE BUG

When his car got dinged, Ron Dolce tried to pretty it up with glued-on marbles. Then he kept going, adding thousands of pieces of stained glass. More than 10,000 marbles later, Dolce has pieced together a quiltlike, solid car: "Its glass skin protects it from sun, wind, or rain."

ART CAR MUSEUM

WHAT: WHIMSICAL WHEELS
WHERE: HOUSTON, TEXAS, U.S.A.

At the Art Car Museum, anything goes! The cars displayed here have been painted, bejeweled, covered in seashells and tin foil, and even adorned with animal heads. Other wacky, wheeled forms of transportation are welcome, too, like a skeleton riding a bone-covered bicycle and a dragster shaped like a high-heeled shoe. Well, that's one way to get around town! (Closed Mondays and Tuesdays.)

MUSIC MACHINE

It's a car! It's a band! It's Pico de Gallo, Blank's salute to Mexican mariachi music. Using brackets, bolts, and superstrong glue, he mounted guitars, drums, a trumpet, a saxophone, an accordion, 300 bells, and other instruments onto an old car. "When you hit a bump, there's a lot of jingling and jangling," Blank says.

DOUBLE TROUBLE

What do you do if you have an extra VW Beetle lying around? Dennis Clay created an art car. The upside-down car is just the car's shell welded around a big pipe. The legs sticking out are mannequins'. "It's only for parades," Clay says. "Above 30 miles an hour (48 km/h), it gets all wiggly."

ROAD SHOW

Wonder what Piet Mondrian, a modern artist, would have thought about this car, which was inspired by the Dutchman's distinctive style? Artist Emily Duffy painted the patterns on the vehicle, then made a matching roof sculpture and clothing. "I want to show people that nothing in life has to be boring," Duffy says.

CRUISE CONTROL

Where other people saw a broken-down junker, artist Rick Worth saw a shipwreck: the *Titanic*. Using plywood and paint, Worth re-created the passenger liner that struck an iceberg and sank in 1912. But this craft has been good luck for some: One couple was married on the "bow" of the car!

HITTING THE ROAD WITH MARISSA GAWEL

Road trip! National Geographic Young Explorer Marissa Gawel recently hit the highways to visit as many roadside attractions as possible. Her mission? To document the sometimes strange, sometimes artsy, and always fun attractions throughout the United States. Four thousand miles (6,437 km) later, Gawel's got plenty of pictures and even more memories of these unique destinations. Here, she shares some of the stories behind her stops.

HAVING A BALL. The wackiest attraction we saw was the world's largest ball of paint in Alexandria, Indiana. It's a baseball covered in about 20,000 layers of paint, and it is as tall as I am. It hangs from the ceiling in its own shed, but it's so big it almost touches the floor. The family started it when their son was three years old. Now he's 35. They gave me a cutting so I could see all the different layers. You'll never see this anywhere else.

FOR THE BIRDS. I loved visiting Bird Paradise in Loogootee, Indiana. A guy named Bill has made thousands of the same birdhouses and displays them in his yard along with lots of twinkle lights, painted rocks, and lawn figurines.

Check it out on page 33!

He was the happiest man we met on the whole trip.

IN GOOD COMPANY. It was great meeting so many people along the way. We would spend two or three hours at each site just talking to them about their work. I didn't anticipate how excited they'd be about sharing their art.

MIRROR, MIRROR. If I were to create my own roadside attraction, it would be a mirror labyrinth in my backyard. A section of the maze would include walls created from mosaics of reflective shards.

SHOW AND TELL. Roadside attractions may not be the best art, but it's inspiring to see people go with their vision and break outside the norm to do their own thing. These attractions bring diversity to the landscape in a very human way.

TAKE A BREAK. If you're going to visit some roadside attractions, give yourself plenty of time to enjoy each site. Don't rush. It's not just about getting the driving done. Set your expectations that the trip will take longer than you think, and you'll make some great memories.

EXPEDITION STOPS

Temple of Tolerance, *Wapakoneta, Ohio*
Jungle Jim's International Market, *Fairfield, Ohio*
Minister's Treehouse, *Crossville, Tennessee*
Salt and Pepper Shaker Museum, *Gatlinburg, Tennessee*
Carolina Hillbilly, *Edneyville, North Carolina*
Old Car City, *White, Georgia*
Paradise Gardens, *Summerville, Georgia*
Pasaquan, *Buena Vista, Georgia*
Museum of Wonder, *Seale, Alabama*
Bamahenge, *Elberta, Alabama*
Abita Mystery House, *Abita Springs, Louisiana*

Margaret's Grocery, *Vicksburg, Mississippi*
Bonnie & Clyde Ambush Museum, *Gibsland, Louisiana*
Fouke's Monster Mart, *Fouke, Arkansas*
Tiny Town Trains, *Hot Springs, Arkansas*
Billy Tripp's Mindfield, *Jackson, Tennessee*
Apple Valley Hillbilly Garden and Toyland, *Calvert City, Kentucky*
Dr. Ted's Musical Marvels, *Dale, Indiana*
Bill Larkin's Bird Paradise, *Loogootee, Indiana*
World's Largest Ball of Paint, *Alexandria, Indiana*

Index

Index

Credits

COVER (UP), Richard Cummins/Getty Images; (CTR LE), Mario Armas/Reuters; (LO LE), Eric Cheng/Barcroft Media/Getty Images; (CTR), Alistair Scott/Alamy; BACK COVER (UP LE), Reuters/Herwig prammer; (LO LE), Hemis/Alamy; (CTR), Dog Bark Park Inn; (RT), John Paul Brooke/REX USA; (LO CTR), Jordan Siemens/Getty Images; 1 (UP), Paul A. Souders/Corbis; 1 (LO), Dennis MacDonald/Alamy Stock Photo; 1 (CTR), Robert Quinlan/Alamy Stock Photo; 2-3 (CTR), Julie Dermansky/Science Source/Getty Images; 4 (LO), UniversalImagesGroup/Getty Images; 4 (UP), Hagen Hopkins/Getty Images; 4 (LO), Universal Images Group/Getty Images; 5 (UP), Catherine Ledner/The Image Bank/Getty Images; 5 (CTR), Rolf Haid/dpa/Corbis; 5 (LO), Aditya "Dicky" Singh/Alamy; 5 (UP RT), REX Shutterstock; 6 (UP), Franck Fotos/Alamy; 6 (CTR), Jim Corwin/Alamy; 6 (LO), Rick Worth/Harrod Blank; 7 (CTR), John Van Decker/Alamy; 8-9, NG Maps; 10 (UP), Gaëtan Rossier/Getty Images; 10 (LO), fototehnik/Shutterstock; 11 (CTR), Arco Images/Scholz, F./Alamy; 12 (UP), Mike Simons/Getty Images; 12 (UP RT), Alan Powdrill/Getty Images; 12 (LO), Nic Hamilton/Alamy; 13 (CTR), Amos Chapple/Rex/REX USA; 14-15 (CTR), Robert Kwiatek/AFP/Getty Images; 16 (CTR), SEPIA/Balan Madhavan/Alamy; 16 (LO LE), Darkroom/Balan Madhavan/Alamy; 17 (UP), Arctic Images/Getty Images; 17 (LO), Courtesy of the Dog Bark Park Inn; 17 (UP LE), Courtesy of Kakslauttanen Arctic Resort; 18 (UP LE), evantravels/Shutterstock; 18 (CTR LE), Hemis/Alamy; 19 (UP), Frank Hoppe/Rex/REX USA; 19 (LO), John Paul Brooke/REX USA; 20 (UP), Diego Giudice/Corbis; 20 (UP LE), Jason Friend/Alamy; 20 (LO), Caters News Agency; 21 (CTR), Alvaro Leiva/Getty Images; 21 (CTR RT), Steve Back/Getty Images; 22 (CTR), Patrick Escudero/Hemis/Corbis; 23 (UP), RoadsideAmerica.com; 23 (LO), RoadsideAmerica.com; 24 (UP), Marissa Gawel; 24 (LO), Rick Rudnicki/Lonely Planet Images/Getty Images; 25 (CTR), Chris Windsor/Getty Images; 26 (UP), Sergei Karpukhin/Reuters; 26 (LO), Mike Greenslade/Australia/Alamy; 26-27, Images-USA/Alamy; 27 (LO), Brian Cahn/ZUMAPRESS.com/Alamy; 28-29 (CTR), Jim Abernethy/National Geographic Creative; 29 (UP), Walter Bibikow/Getty Images; 29 (LO), Richard Cummins/Alamy; 30 (UP), James Quine/Alamy; 30 (LO), Brendan Farrington/AP Photo; 31 (CTR), Franck Fotos/Alamy; 32 (CTR), RoadsideAmerica.com; 32 (LO CTR), William Leaman/Alamy; 33 (LO), Marissa Gawel; 33 (UP), RoadsideAmerica.com; 33 (CTR

RT), Marissa Gawel; 34 (UP), incamerastock/Alamy; 34 (LO), Hagen Hopkins/Getty Images Entertainment; 35 (CTR), Franck Fotos/Alamy; 36 (LO), Craig Tuttle/Corbis/Alamy; 37 (UP), Pawel Toczynski/Getty Images; 37 (LO), Universal Images Group/Getty Images; 38-39, Damien McFadden Photography Limited/Rex/REX USA; 38 (LO), Bob Strong/Reuters; 39 (LO), RoadsideAmerica.com; 40 (CTR RT), Reuters/Herwig Prammer; 40 (LO), Reuters/Herwig Prammer; 41 (CTR), Reuters; 42 (CTR), Susana Gonzalez/Corbis; 42 (LO), Design Pics Inc./Alamy; 43 (UP), Laszlo Balogh/Reuters; 44 (CTR), www.corsozundert.nl/Rex/REX USA; 45 (UP), Raul Arboleda/Getty Images; 45 (LO), Andrew Winning/Reuters; 46-47 (CTR), image-BROKER/Alamy; 46 (LO LE), imageBROKER/Alamy; 48 (UP LE), Tom Bean/Alamy; 48 (LO), Richard Cummins/Lonely Planet Images/Getty Images; 49 (LO), Paul Carter/Alamy; 50 (UP), Hemis/Alamy; 50 (LO), Michael Jenner/Alamy; 51 (RT), Charles Cook/Getty Images; 52 (UP), Courtesy of Alex Ludden; 52 (LO), Courtesy of Alex Ludden; 53 (UP), Paul Kitagaki Jr./Sacramento Bee/ZUMAPRESS/Alamy; 53 (LO), Zuma Press Inc./Alamy; 54 (UP LE), Maurice Crooks/Alamy; 54 (UP RT), Lebrecht Music and Arts Photo Library/Alamy; 54 (LO), Tony McNicol/Alamy; 55 (CTR and LO), Unclaimed Baggage Center; 56 (CTR), Portland Press Herald/Getty Images; 56 (LO LE), Portland Press Herald/Getty Images; 57 (CTR), Franck Fotos/Alamy; 57 (RT), Franck Fotos/Alamy; 58 (CTR), Bob Pardue - Signs/Alamy; 59 (UP RT), Denise Panyik-Dale/Getty Images; 59 (LO LE), Don Smetzer/Alamy; 60 (UP LE), joel zatz/Alamy; 60 (LO), epa european pressphoto agency b.v./Alamy; 61 (CTR), Melissa Gawel; 62 (CTR), Robert Quinlan/Alamy; 63 (UP LE), dmac/Alamy; 63 (CTR RT), Travel Images/UIG/Getty Images; 63 (LO LE), Dennis MacDonald/Alamy; 64 (CTR), Louis Berticevich, Mystery Spot; 65 (CTR), Lynn Palmer/Alamy; 65 (LO), cs333/Shutterstock; 66 (CTR), Jim Corwin/Alamy; 66-67 (CTR), David Barnes/DanitaDelimont.com; 68 (CTR), Franck Fotos/Alamy; 69 (UP), Hale-Sutton Europe/Alamy; 69 (LO), Doug Kirby/Roadside America; 70 (UP RT), Czarek Sokolowski/AP Photo; 70 (LO LE), ZUMA Press Inc./Alamy; 70 (CTR), ZUMA Press Inc./Alamy; 70 (UP RT), Alik Keplicz/AP Photo; 71 (UP), Andrew Woodley/Alamy; 71 (LO), Courtesy of the Santa Claus House; 72 (UP), Robert Shantz/Alamy; 72 (LO), David Ghysels; 73 (CTR), RGB Ventures/SuperStock/Alamy; 74 (CTR),

Reuters; 75 (UP), Chris Heurich/Alamy; 75 (LO LE), Michael Robertson/Alamy; 75 (INSET), Ted Kinsman/Science Source; 76 (CTR), Hemis/Alamy; 77 (UP), Danita Delimont/Alamy; 77 (LO), Paul Biris/Moment/Getty Images; 78 (UP), Jamie Carstairs/Alamy; 78 (LO), Itar Tass/Yuri Belinsky/Newscom; 79 (CTR), LatitudeStock/Alamy; 80 (CTR), Gary Doak/Alamy; 81 Jack Sullivan/Alamy; 82 (UP), The Protected Art Archive/Alamy; 82 (LO), Yasuyoshi Chiba/AFP/Getty Images; 83 (CTR), Alistair Scott/Alamy; 84 (UP LE), Franck Fotos/Alamy; 84 (LO), Steve Outram/Alamy; 85 (CTR), Paul A. Souders/Corbis; 86 (CTR), Fabrizio Bensch/Reuters; 87 (UP), Andy Clark/Reuters; 87 (LO), Rolf Haid/dpa/Corbis; 88 (CTR), dave stamboulis/Alamy; 88 (CTR), Matthew Brady/Buyenlarge/Getty Images; 89 (CTR), Ian G Dagnall/Alamy; 89, Stephan Hoerold/Getty Images; 90 (CTR), Aditya "Dicky" Singh/Alamy; 91 (CTR), Reuters/Oswaldo Rivas; 91 (LO RT), Boonchuay Promjiam/Shutterstock; 92 (CTR), Scott Warren/Alamy; 92 (LO), Buddy Mays/Alamy; 93 (CTR), George H. H. Huey/Alamy; 94 (UP), Marissa Gawel; 94 (LO), Jack Sullivan/Alamy; 94 (UP RT), Penn Greene; 95 (CTR), The Asahi Shimbun/Getty Images; 96 (UP LE), Gina Kelly/Alamy; 96 (UP RT), Franck Fotos/Alamy; 96 (LO LE), Wu Wei/Xinhua Press/Corbis; 97 (CTR), Rex/Rex USA; 98 (CTR), ZUMA Press, Inc./Alamy; 99 (UP), LOOK Die Bildagentur der Fotografen GmbH/Alamy; 99 (LO), Stuart Miles/Dreamstime; 100-101 (LE), Olivier Chouchana/Gamma-Rapho/Getty Images; 101 (UP), AP Photo/Jonathan Browning/Rex Features; 101 (LO), AP Photo/Jonathan Browning/Rex Features; 102 (CTR), Qilai Shen/EPA/Newscom; 103 (CTR), ChinaFotoPress/Getty Images; 103 (LO LE), Olivier Chouchana/Gamma-Rapho/Getty Images; 104 (CTR), Olivier Chouchana/Gamma-Rapho/Getty Images; 104-105, f11photo/Shutterstock; 106 (LO LE), Danita Delimont/Alamy; 106-107, Hunter Mann/Harrod Blank; 106 (CTR), Ron Dolce/Harrod Blank; 106 (UP), Bob Castaneda/Harrod Blank; 107 (UP LE), Dennis Clay/Harrod Blank; 107 (UP RT), Emily Duffy/Harrod Blank; 107 (CTR RT), Rick Worth/Harrod Blank; 108 (UP CTR LE), Mark Thiessen/NGS; 108 (UP), Marissa Gawel; 112, Dave Stamboulis/Alamy

Since 1888, the National Geographic Society has funded more than 12,000 research, exploration, and preservation projects around the world. The Society receives funds from National Geographic Partners LLC, funded in part by your purchase. A portion of the proceeds from this book supports this vital work.

For more information, visit www.natgeo.com, call 1-800-647-5463, or write to the following address:
National Geographic Partners, LLC
1145 17th Street N.W.
Washington, D.C. 20036-4688 U.S.A.

Visit us online at nationalgeographic.com/books

For librarians and teachers: ngchildrensbooks.org

More for kids from National Geographic:
kids.nationalgeographic.com

For information about special discounts for bulk purchases, please contact National Geographic Books Special Sales: ngspecsales@ngs.org

For rights or permissions inquiries, please contact National Geographic Books Subsidiary Rights: ngbookrights@ngs.org

NATIONAL GEOGRAPHIC and Yellow Border Design are trademarks of the National Geographic Society, used under license.

Art Director: Callie Broaddus
Designer: Simon Renwick

The publisher wishes to acknowledge the writers for this book: Kristin Baird Rattini, Kay Boatner, Elisabeth Deffner, Kait Gallagher, Kitson Jazynka, Jamie Kiffel-Alcheh, Emily Krieger, Molly Marcot, Sean McCollum, Michael Monahan, Jen Rini, Amanda Sandlin, B. F. Summers, C. M. Tomlin, Sarah Youngson.

Library of Congress Cataloging-in-Publication Data

Title: 125 wacky roadside attractions.
Other titles: One hundred twenty five wacky roadside attractions
Description: Washington, DC: National Geographic, 2016. | Includes index. |
  Audience: 8-12.
Identifiers: LCCN 2015041335| ISBN 9781426324079 (pbk. : alk. paper) | ISBN
  9781426324086 (library binding : alk. paper)
Subjects: LCSH: Automobile travel--Guidebooks--Juvenile literature. |
  Curiosities and wonders--Guidebooks--Juvenile literature.
Classification: LCC G153.4 .A1554 2016 | DDC 910.4--dc23
LC record available at http://lccn.loc.gov/2015041335

Printed in Hong Kong
16/THK/1

page 88